Merry Christmas
Jill
2003

MW00814454

Merry Christmas
Jill

Cooking & Entertaining with Beer

Rob Driver

ProSe Associates, Inc.
HIGHLANDS RANCH, COLORADO

COOKING AND ENTERTAINING WITH BEER

By Rob Driver

Publisher & Editor:	Joseph W. Mierzwa
Copy Editor:	Mary Petri West
Design:	Dorothy Kavka
Typesetting:	Daniel F. Lillian
Photography:	Rolana C. Mierzwa
Photo Assistant:	Sherri Driver
Food Stylist:	Rolana C. Mierzwa

Place settings and accessories provided courtesy of Pier 1 Imports.

All brand names and product names included in this book are the trademarks, registered trademarks, or trade names of their respective holders.

Published by

ProSe Associates, Inc.

P.O. BOX 4333, HIGHLANDS RANCH, COLORADO 80126

ISBN: 0-9637285-2-0

Library of Congress Catalog Number: 95-61719

Printed in USA

10 9 8 7 6 5 4 3 2 1

Acknowledgements

$\mathscr{I}$ would like to thank the following people for sharing their tried and true family recipes for use in this book: Jim and Donna Driver, Harriet Bain, Ruby Siegman, Laura Arceneaux, Karen Agee, Alice Stephens, Chris Ragaisis, and Liz Kaessner.

A special thank you goes to my family, Sherri, Ryan, and Reanna, for their patience, trust, and tactful critiques while I tested many recipe variations on the family (all of whom are still alive).

I give a grateful "thank you" to Dana Rosebrook for her professional editing and word processing assistance.

Also, thanks to Sue Dubach at The Cooking School of the Rockies for proving that simpler is often better (some recipes just have too darn many unnecessary steps and ingredients!) and her inspiration to be creative… let no recipe stand untouched.

Table of Contents

Introduction

This book has something for anyone who eats food, hosts parties, or drinks beer. If you have never cooked with beer, this book will open your eyes to a whole new world of taste possibilities. If you have already dabbled in beer cookery, it will broaden your horizons and offer new challenges for the taste buds. If you already know how to use beer in cooking, this book is a baseline for you to make individualized modifications and develop a personal repertoire of exceptional beer recipes.

For anyone who wants to have a unique party which capitalizes on the recent explosion in high-quality beers and beer varieties, there are menus, recommendations, and guidelines for holding social events which will delight your friends and family. This includes details on party theme ideas, beer handling, purchasing, identification, judging, and even a checklist for holding your own beer-tasting session.

If you are intrigued and excited by the different styles of beers available, this book contains information to help you hone your beer-tasting skills. You can increase your appreciation of beer flavors by reviewing the section on beer styles and following the beer-tasting guidelines. Beer-judging terminology and a representative judging form are also included.

For the cook who wants to find just what is needed for a special occasion, all recipes are extensively cross-referenced. There is a standard alphabetical index of recipes, but you can also look through another index for recipes that use the beer styles you prefer or that you already have on hand. If you want to look for recipes that use particular main ingredients that may be available (either on sale or on hand), you can refer to the main ingredient index. And if you only have a set amount of time available for cooking, use the preparation time index.

So whether you plan to use food to enhance the taste of beer or use beer to enhance the taste of food, there is something here for you. Above all, be bold, innovative, and have fun with the world's oldest beverage and its nearly universal application to exceptional cooking and entertaining.

Beer
An Overview

Beer is a simple fermented beverage with thousands of years of history and nearly infinite varieties. The basic ingredients are unchanging: water, grain, hops, and yeast. Water comprises 90% of beer and serves as the liquid medium for the other ingredients. Grains are processed by soaking and heating to create the sugars which ferment into alcohol. Hops are the flowers of the hops plant which are added at various stages to create aromas, flavor, and/or bitterness and, to some extent, act as a preservative. Yeast is the microorganism that converts the fermentable sugars to alcohol and carbon dioxide.

Brewing, the craft of making beer, starts with converting a grain to fermentable sugar. Barley, the most common brewing grain, is germinated, sprouted, and dried to create "malted" barley. The starches in malted barley (and other grain starches such as wheat, corn, and rice) are converted to sugar when they are mixed and heated in water. The resultant "mash" is strained to extract the liquid from the spent grain. This liquid is combined with hops and boiled. After removing the hops, the liquid "wort" is cooled to an appropriate temperature and the beer yeast is added, starting the fermentation process. Within several days, the yeast has converted fermentable sugars to alcohol and carbon dioxide; any carbon dioxide trapped in the beer provides carbonation for the resultant product. After storage at cool temperatures (days to months, depending on the style), the finished beer is packaged for delivery to the happy beer drinker.

Much like bread, a nearly inexhaustible list of beer varieties can be made by using slightly different versions and combinations of just a few simple ingredients. The grains can be heated to varying degrees, even burned, resulting in a range of colors and flavors in the final product. The amount of sugar which is fermentable can be varied to modify sweetness and alcohol content. Hops come in a wide variety, providing a range of bitterness, aroma, and flavor. Beer yeast has numerous varieties used in fermentation at temperatures which can range from 33 to 70 degrees Fahrenheit. In addition to influencing the fermentation process, some yeasts add flavors all their own to the beer. Small quantities of special items (such as fruit) can be added to the brewing process to create even more diversity.

Beer Styles

"Beer" is a comprehensive term encompassing several families of fermented beverage: lagers, ales, and hybrid beers. The brewing process differentiates between ales and lagers by the different yeasts used and the fermentation temperatures. Lager is brewed with a special yeast (called bottom-fermenting) and is fermented at temperatures between 33 and 50 degrees. Most lager beers are stored at low temperatures for weeks to months resulting in a typically smooth, crisp flavor. The term "lagern" actually means "to store" in German. Although most American taste buds associate lager with a light, blonde-colored, medium strength beer, a lager is identified strictly by the brewing process and the result can be any color, bitterness, or strength. Ales are traditionally brewed with ale yeast (called top-fermenting) and fermented at temperatures of 60 to 70 degrees, resulting in a rougher and more complex flavor profile. Hybrid, or mixed-style, beers blend characteristics and brewing techniques of both top- and bottom-fermented beer styles. Hybrids can also result from the creative use of additional flavoring ingredients.

There are about 60 different beer styles recognized for national brewing competitions. The styles listed here summarize many of those categories, grouping similar styles together under one name. Use this list as a guide for the major category distinctions for your beer-tasting and cooking, but be aware that there are many subcategories and alternative ways to describe beer. Charlie Papazian, President of the Association of Brewers, suggests that there are so many different combinations of brewing techniques and ingredients that we may need an informal category called "just beer." (*Zymurgy,* Vol. 14, No. 1, Spring 1991, page 5)

PALE ALE

This style is characteristically dry with a noticeable hops aroma and bitterness. "Pale" refers to the color of the beer in comparison to the darker ales. The classic English pale ales are brewed from very hard water, which lends itself to the use of more hops.

INDIA PALE ALE

This style's origin dates to the long transits from Britain to India in the nineteenth century. Since hops are an excellent preservative and alcohol helps to kill bacteria, both were used generously in the beers to be transported by sailing ship to India. The resultant beer style is stronger and hoppier than pale ale and typically has a flowery aroma.

BITTER

The traditional English pub drink. This is basically a pale ale style, but having a balanced malt/hops taste with very low carbonation. It is called "bitter" to indicate its stronger hops character compared to the "mild" brown ales. A bitter can be "ordinary," "special," or "extra special" ("ESB"), each version having increasing hops strength, body, and alcohol content over the previous one.

BROWN ALE

A traditional sweet, malty British beer style, rather dark, mildly-hopped and low in alcohol. Mild brown ale was brewed as a thirst-quencher for the working classes in the early northern England mills, hence the need for a lower alcohol beverage.

BELGIAN ALES

Although there are hundreds of styles of beers from Belgium, those most commonly available in the U.S. are Flanders Brown ales, Trappist ales, Saison, and Lambics (e.g., Faro, Gueuze, Kriek, Framboise). All are characteristically sour and dry with complex fruity overtones. Lambics are spontaneously fermented with indigenous airborne wild yeast by leaving the wort open to the elements.

SCOTCH ALE

A style with a misleading name, since it originated in France. It is generally a strong beer with an overwhelmingly malty taste, residual sweetness, and little hops aroma or bitterness. It can be ordered in Scotland (and other places) by asking for a "wee heavy." "Scottish" ales are less full-bodied and malty than strong Scotch ales and are often grouped with the English bitter category.

PORTER

A very dark, nearly black beer with a dry, coffee-like, almost bittersweet flavor. The character comes from the use of dark malts rather than roasted barley as in stouts. Named for its popularity among the porters and other working men in eighteenth century London.

STOUT

A very dark (opaque), full-bodied beer with roasted, almost chocolatey flavor. They are typically low in alcohol content with the dark rich color coming from roasted unmalted barley. This style includes dry stout (Irish style), sweet stout (sometimes using milk sugar), and oatmeal stout (a rich, smooth flavor from the addition of oats).

IMPERIAL STOUT

This is a heavy, well-hopped, relatively sweet variant of stout with high alcohol content, typically exceeding 8%. Originally brewed for the Russian Imperial Court of Catherine the Great. The high alcohol and hops were designed to provide survivability during transport.

BARLEYWINE

An ale with extremely high alcohol content, approaching that of wine (13%). Barley-wine is a full-bodied, bittersweet beer with a color ranging from copper to dark brown.

Lagers

PILSENER

This style is the model for pale lagers worldwide, being well-hopped and medium bodied with little malt flavor. Its name derives from the city where it was originally brewed—Plzen, Czechoslovakia. A version of Pilsener is by far the most common beer style among U.S. breweries. The American variation typically has higher carbonation with considerably less hop bitterness and body and often uses other ingredients such as corn and rice with the malted barley in the brewing process. European, or Continental, Pilsener lies somewhere between the original Pilsener style and the American version, having a little more hops, body, and alcohol than its American counterpart.

MUNICH HELLES

A lighter version of the basic Munich style, Munich Helles has robust maltiness and relatively low alcohol content and bitterness. It is the standard daily fare in southern Germany.

AMBER

These beers are fairly strong, typically reddish-brown to copper colored and have a distinct malty taste and aroma with a light, clean hops bitterness. Vienna and Marzen/Oktoberfest are classic examples of the amber lager style.

EXPORT

Also known as Dortmunder style, this is a relatively strong, medium-bodied pale lager. It has a higher alcohol content than Pilsener and is more aggressively hopped than amber lager styles. It is called "export" because it was purposely brewed with higher alcohol and hops to withstand the rigors of shipping. The term also has other meanings; see the section below on "Other Style Terminology."

DARK LAGER

Dark lagers typically have a dominant malty flavor and aroma, resulting from the use of dark roasted malts. Munich Dunkel is the basic model for dark ("dunkel") lagers, fairly full-bodied with an almost bread-like aroma. The lagering process (cold storage) produces a crisp, clean beer with less sweetness and more hops and carbonation than a brown ale. The American version has less pronounced maltiness and higher carbonation.

BOCK

A strong, malty, fairly sweet lager with moderate hops bitterness, usually deep copper to brown colored. A "helles" (pale) bock has a similar flavor profile but is made almost entirely with light-colored malted barley.

DOPPELBOCK

This is a stronger version of the bock beer, similar in almost all respects except alcohol content. A doppelbock usually can be identified by the suffix "-ator" on its name, i.e., "Terminator" and "Kulminator."

Hybrid Styles

ALT

A German top-fermented beer, usually strongly hopped, with medium malt taste and moderate alcohol content. "Alt" means old, meant to distinguish it in Germany from the newer style, lager.

CREAM ALE

A unique combination of warm (top or bottom) fermentation and cold lagering. A mild, pale, light-bodied beer.

WHEAT BEERS

A distinctively German variation, these are usually top-fermented and cold lagered, using from 25% to 70% wheat instead of barley. A tart, fruity, lightly hopped, fairly carbonated lager, often with a clove- or nutmeg-like flavor. These beers often receive a final fermentation in the bottle, called bottle conditioning ("hefe-weizen") creating yeast sediment. "Weizen/Weissbier" beer is made with at least 25% wheat in the malt composition and a "Berliner Weisse" is brewed using wheat for as much as two-thirds of the grain. Dunkelweizen is a darker version with more malt flavor; weizenbock is a higher alcohol wheat beer with more malty sweetness.

SPECIALTY

This category is a class of beer brewed using any fermentable ingredients other than malted barley; examples of "other" ingredients are honey, syrup, sorghum, and malted rye. This category also includes beers brewed with unusual techniques, such as "steinbier," a beer style created by heating porous stones and placing them in the beer wort before fermentation. They are then removed and cooled, leaving a coating of sugars crystallized on the stones. The stones are returned to the beer during fermentation and the yeast converts the crystallized sugars, leaving an unusual caramel, smoky taste.

STEAM BEER

This is an amber lager brewed at ale fermentation temperatures, producing a strong hop character and substantial body. This is really the only beer style indigenous to America; Anchor Brewing Company uses "Steam Beer" as a trademarked name.

RAUCHBIER

The name translates as "smoked beer," the unusual character usually imparted by drying or lightly roasting the malt under smoky conditions, often using smoldering beechwood chips.

HERB BEER

This style is produced by using herbs or spices, such as ginger, coriander, pumpkin pie spices, or ginseng instead of hops to create flavors. Since spicy overtones are a typical characteristic, Christmas or holiday beers could be included in this category.

CHRISTMAS BEER

Many breweries produce a special beer for the holiday season, typically a full-bodied, well-flavored ale or lager. Many have nutmeg or other spices added. While this is not really a unique beer style, the seasonal winter beers tend to have similar characteristics and can serve as an interesting theme for a holiday beer-tasting.

FRUIT BEER

A beer made with fruit as an adjunct. It may be added during the primary fermentation or afterwards to produce a second, separate fermentation. Some of the fruits which have been used include cherries, cranberries, apricots, lemon, passion fruit, and raspberries.

CHILI BEER

This is basically a Pilsener-style lager with jalapeno, Anaheim, serrano, or other hot chilies added to the brew.

Other Style Terminology

DRY BEER

This is a genetically engineered beer with an alcohol content slightly higher than regular beer. By altering the yeast strain used, normally unfermentable dextrins are changed into fermentable sugars. The "dry" taste results from the lack of sugar in the final brew (the sugar having been almost entirely converted to alcohol).

ICE BEER

The alcohol content of this beer is increased by cooling the brew just below the freezing point of water, but still well above the freezing point of alcohol. After removing some of the ice, the resultant beer has a relatively higher proportion of alcohol without having changed the basic fermentation process.

LIGHT

The term "light" on a beer label can refer to one of two things, the color or the calories. When used to indicate color, it is intended to distinguish the paler versions of a brand (usually European) from their dark beers. According to the FDA, when the term is used in reference to calories, "light" beers must have at least 25% fewer calories than the regular version of that beer.

MALT LIQUOR

This term on a label is more descriptive of state laws regulating alcohol content than the beer style. State laws vary, but many require that a beer with alcohol content greater than 5% by weight must be called either malt liquor, ale, stout, or porter. This restrictive labeling clearly prevents adequate identification of the vast majority of beer styles. A beer labeled "malt liquor" can be an ale, lager, or hybrid style that happens to have an alcohol content exceeding a state threshold.

EXPORT

The label "export" can be used in ways that are totally unrelated to beer style; it can be applied to beers to denote a version which is intended for consumption outside the brewing country or sometimes is merely used as a marketing device to imply higher quality.

PALE LAGER

This is a catch-all term for light-colored lagers. It generally encompasses Pilseners (including the American and European variations), export (Dortmunder), and Munich Helles.

Cooking

*I*n this section, you will learn the ways that you can combine beer and food to achieve higher states of cooking excellence and enjoyment. The different methods of using beer and some substitution guidelines are provided so that you can create your own personalized dishes. This section also includes luscious recipes for appetizers, main dishes, side dishes, soups, salsas, sauces, dressings, and breads, all using beer.

⟞⟡⟝

Beer in the Kitchen

Beer is one of those versatile ingredients whose range of characteristics makes diverse contributions to the art of cooking. It can marinate, flavor, moisten, tenderize, season, or serve as the base in a recipe, to be embellished by the addition of other ingredients. The extremely broad range of beer styles provides an opportunity for the cook to achieve a variety of flavors: malty sweetness, the bitterness of hops, subtle fruity over-tones, or sharp spicy sensations, depending on the beer chosen. The discussion of beer cookery in this section and the recipes are merely the tip of the iceberg—innovate, explore, and enjoy!

⟜ Beer is a fine ingredient for a marinade. A marinade, used to flavor foods before cooking, is typically a liquid composed of acid and oil. A standard marinade uses a ratio of three parts oil to one part acid, plus desired seasonings. Almost any oil can be used and wheat beer is a particularly effective acidic ingredient.

⟜ Soups and stews gain a new dimension in flavor by using different beers as part of the basic liquid.

⟜ Beer has often been called "liquid bread"; the combination of the two will enhance the full-bodied grain and yeasty flavors inherent in each. The beer/bread affinity can also be exploited by using beer instead of water to moisten stuffing.

ᗧᒣ Braising is a cooking method using moist heat to tenderize and flavor meats. The meat is first seared in a small amount of hot fat, then a cooking liquid is added, brought to a simmer, and allowed to cook until the meat is done. When used as the cooking liquid, beer provides tenderizing qualities as well as a flavorful sauce.

ᗧᒣ Use beer like a table seasoning to achieve a delightful new flavor in existing dishes. Try a splash of chili beer with a salsa or a Lambic over sliced fruit.

ᗧᒣ Beer can be the flavor base for vinaigrettes and sauces. Substitute a well-hopped Pilsener for the vinegar in a dressing or make a barbecue sauce with a rich dark lager beer.

In addition to providing an important base ingredient in many existing recipes, beer can be creatively substituted, offering a bright new array of cooking options derived from your own recipes. You can replace up to one-fourth of the water in a soup recipe with beer. Substitute beer for the cooking oil when sautéing vegetables (use about twice as much beer as oil called for in the recipe and keep stirring to avoid burning). Replace all or part of the acid in a marinade or dressing with beer, one-for-one, preferably using a wheat beer or Belgian ale. Because of the similarities in their brewing processes, beer can be an excellent one-for-one substitute for vinegar in some recipes. Wherever a recipe calls for fruit juice, sherry, or wine, try an appropriate beer for some or all of the amount. Consider a rich, malty beer as an equivalent replacement for up to one-third of the tomato sauce in a recipe. Beer can also be a one-for-one substitute for as much as three-fourths of the water in some bread recipes.

Beer can add bitterness when substituted in an existing recipe, so consider a small increase in the amount of sugar in the recipe. It is generally not advisable to substitute beer for liquid in recipes that call for reduction, a process that removes some or all of the water in a liquid, thereby thickening as well as concentrating the liquid's flavor. Concentrating beer through reduction can result in an overpowering bitter taste.

In most dishes (except breads), it doesn't matter if the beer is warm or cold when added. If a beer has been opened, use it as quickly as possible to avoid the off-tastes that come from oxidation.

If you are concerned about the alcohol content of the resulting food, focus on the dishes which require cooking after addition of the beer. Since it has a lower boiling point than water, the alcohol in beer will tend to evaporate during the cooking process, leaving flavor but little or no residual alcohol. Beer added after or without cooking, as in some soups and sauces, will retain its alcoholic content.

If you would like some ideas for different beers to use as you begin making your own recipe modifications or additions, you will find some general beer/food combination suggestions in Chapter Five.

Recipes

This section provides recipes for main dishes, side dishes, appetizers, soups, breads and accompaniments which contain beer as an ingredient. All of these recipes use beer to enhance or add pleasant new flavors. For this reason, a dessert section is not included, since (at least in my opinion) there are few dessert recipes to which beer makes a positive contribution.

There are some conventions used in the descriptions of ingredients.

~ When herbs and spices are used, the recipe calls for a dried version unless otherwise noted. Herbs that are available in powdered form, e.g., thyme, should be used at half the rate of the dried leaf version, if at all.

~ Cheese quantities will be described as ounces when a chunk is to be used and in terms of cups when it is grated. Three ounces of cheddar or Monterey Jack yields about one cup when grated.

~ When a recipe calls for a certain volume (e.g. ½ cup) of an ingredient that is chopped, diced, minced, or sliced, measure the amount after chopping, dicing, mincing or slicing.

~ One stick of butter is 8 tablespoons or ½ cup.

~ When one "chicken breast" is called for in the recipe, it is actually half of an entire chicken's breast. Since they are typically divided into half-breast pieces for sale, that is the increment used here.

~ Unless otherwise stated, an "onion" means a medium-sized yellow or white onion.

~ All-purpose flour is acceptable in all recipes that call for flour, unless otherwise specified.

~ All peppers (green bell, red bell, jalapeno, or serrano) are presumed to be seeded before use in the recipe.

~ When chicken or beef stock is called for, use soup stock from bones if you have it, or canned broth or bouillon as an acceptable substitute.

~ Even though it is typically available in 12 ounce bottles, beer quantities are referenced in terms of cups. So unless the recipe calls for exactly one and one half cups of beer, it may become necessary to drink the remainder while cooking. Another occupational hazard.

Appetizers

HUMMUS

2 cans	garbanzo beans (15½ oz. cans)
1 tsp	lemon juice
2 cloves	garlic, chopped
1 tsp	sesame seeds
¼ cup	dark lager (or chili beer, if you like it spicier)
1 tsp	coriander
1 tsp	cumin
¼ tsp	cayenne
½ tsp	salt

Drain chickpeas. Combine all ingredients in food processor until smooth. Add more beer if necessary to achieve desired consistency. Serve as dip for vegetables or on crackers.

Makes about 3 cups.

CEVICHE

1 lb.	white fish fillets, boneless, cut in ½" strips
1 cup	wheat beer
1 cup	lime juice
3 Tbsp	olive oil
1	large tomato, chopped
2 Tbsp	fresh cilantro, chopped
3	green onions, chopped
1	large jalapeno, minced
1 tsp	salt
10	green olives, pitted, chopped

Marinate fish overnight in beer and lime juice in glass or ceramic bowl. Drain off all but about 1 Tbsp liquid. Add other ingredients and mix well.

Serves 4-6.

MARINATED MUSHROOMS

1 lb.	mushrooms
¾ cup	Italian salad dressing
¼ cup	rauchbier
1 Tbsp	parsley, minced
¼ tsp	black pepper
1 dash	liquid hot pepper sauce

Rinse mushrooms thoroughly and trim stem ends. Combine other ingredients in bowl and add mushrooms. Let stand at room temperature for 6-8 hours, stirring occasionally.

Serves 8.

BEER-BATTERED OYSTERS

½ cup	cornmeal
¼ cup	white flour, unbleached
½ cup	milk
1	egg
¼ cup	dark lager
12-16	oysters, freshly shucked
¼ cup	vegetable oil

Combine cornmeal, flour, milk, egg and beer to make batter. Do not over-mix. Refrigerate for at least 30 minutes before using. Heat oil in heavy skillet until hot, about 375°. Dip oysters in batter and place carefully in skillet, cooking until golden brown on all sides. Remove from oil and drain on paper towels.

Serves 4-6.

IPA CHEESE BALL

3 cups	sharp cheddar, grated
1½ cups	Swiss cheese, grated
4 oz.	cream cheese, softened
¼ cup	pecan pieces
1	onion, chopped
¼ cup	parsley, chopped
¼ cup	India Pale Ale
1 dash	liquid hot pepper sauce

Combine all ingredients in food processor and process until smooth. Mold to desired shape and chill. Serve with crackers or bread.

Serves about 12.

MEXICAN CHICKEN APPETIZERS

6	chicken breasts, boneless, skinless
2 Tbsp	fresh cilantro, chopped
1	jalapeno, minced
1½ Tbsp	soy sauce
¾ cup	dark lager
1 Tbsp	lime juice
10	bamboo skewers, soaked in water for 30 minutes

Combine all ingredients except chicken in glass bowl. Cut chicken breasts into 1" cubes, add to marinade, cover, and marinate in the refrigerator for 1-2 hours. Remove chicken cubes from marinade, string on cooking skewers and broil or grill until cooked through, about 4-5 minutes total, turning once.

Serves 8-10.

CHEESE DIP

1 lb.	processed pasteurized cheese, cubed
2	large tomatoes, seeded, drained, chopped
4 oz. can	chilies, diced
6 Tbsp	bitter
1 Tbsp	fresh cilantro, chopped

Combine all ingredients in saucepan and stir together over low heat until cheese is melted. Serve with chips, vegetables, or crackers.

Serves 6-8.

PORTER STEAMED CLAMS

1 cup	porter
4 cloves	garlic, chopped
3 lbs.	clams, scrubbed and rinsed
¼ cup	fresh parsley, chopped

Bring porter and garlic to a boil in heavy pot with a lid. Add clams, cover, and steam until clams open, about 7-9 minutes. Discard any clams that don't open. Remove clams to serving dish. Stir parsley into pot liquid and pour over clams.

Serves 8.

SWEET AND SOUR MEATBALLS

2 lbs.	ground beef or ground chuck
2	eggs, beaten slightly
¾ cup	bread cubes, soft
1½ cups	catsup
¼ cup	brown sugar, tightly packed
2 Tbsp	vinegar
3 Tbsp	pale ale
3 Tbsp	soy sauce

Mix ground meat, eggs, and bread together well. Roll into 1" balls. Brown on all sides in frying pan; drain. In separate bowl, combine catsup, brown sugar, vinegar, pale ale, and soy sauce. Pour sauce over meatballs in frying pan and simmer for about 30 minutes, stirring occasionally to coat meatballs well.

Makes about 50 meatballs.

HOT CLAM DIP

1	large onion, chopped
1	green bell pepper, chopped
6 Tbsp	butter
8 oz.	minced clams (two 4 oz. cans), drained
1 lb.	pasteurized processed cheese, cubed
½ cup	catsup
2 Tbsp	Worcestershire sauce
3 Tbsp	stout
½ tsp	cayenne

Sauté onion and green pepper in butter until soft. Add to the top of a double boiler along with the remainder of the ingredients. Heat until cheese is melted, stirring often. Serve with chips, crackers or crisp bread.

Makes about 2½ cups.

GRILLED SHRIMP

½ cup	India Pale Ale
⅓ cup	sesame oil
⅓ cup	soy sauce
½ tsp	sugar
¼ tsp	garlic powder
¼ tsp	ground ginger
2 lbs.	shrimp, peeled and deveined
10	bamboo skewers, soaked in water for 30 minutes

Combine all ingredients except shrimp in a glass or ceramic bowl. Add shrimp and stir gently. Refrigerate for 2-3 hours. String shrimp on skewers and grill until opaque, 8-10 minutes.

Serves 8-10.

CHEESE STICKS

1 cup	flour
¼ cup	sesame seeds
1 cup	sharp cheddar cheese, grated
½ tsp	salt
½ tsp	sugar
½ tsp	ground ginger
1	egg yolk, beaten
2 Tbsp	bock beer
½ tsp	Worcestershire sauce
⅓ cup	butter, melted

Combine all dry ingredients together in a bowl. Stir in the remainder of the ingredients and form into a soft ball. Chill in refrigerator for 30 minutes. Roll out between two sheets of wax paper, forming a slab about ¼" thick. Cut into strips (at least ½" wide) or any other shape desired. Bake on cookie sheet at 350° for about 10 minutes—do not brown.

Makes about 45 three-inch sticks.

BEDDAR CHEDDAR SPREAD

3 cups	cheddar cheese, grated
½ cup	steam beer
¾ tsp	garlic powder
¼ tsp	liquid hot pepper
1 Tbsp	Worcestershire sauce
½ tsp	dry mustard
1 Tbsp	parsley

Combine all ingredients in food processor at low speed. Serve with crackers, bread or chips.

Makes about 2½ cups.

Soups

REFRIED BEAN SOUP

28 oz. can	crushed tomatoes, with liquid
1 clove	garlic, minced
1	onion, finely chopped
1 cup	Amber lager
30 oz. can	refried beans, any variety
2 cups	chicken broth
1 Tbsp	cilantro, chopped
¼ cup	sour cream

Combine tomatoes, garlic, onion, and beer in large saucepan; boil 5 minutes, stirring often. Stir in beans and broth; simmer over low heat for 20 minutes, stirring occasionally. Serve with dollop of sour cream and sprinkle of cilantro in each bowl.

Serves 6.

CURRIED MUSHROOM SOUP

1 Tbsp	vegetable oil
2-3	medium leeks, sliced, white part only
2 Tbsp	flour
1 Tbsp	curry powder
4 cups	milk
1 tsp	chicken bouillon granules
7 cups	chopped mushrooms, such as portobello, shiitake, morel, porcini, etc., chopped
3 Tbsp	India Pale Ale

Heat vegetable oil in large heavy saucepan or Dutch oven. Add leeks and sauté until soft, about 4 minutes. Add flour and curry powder and stir to coat leeks. Stir in milk and chicken bouillon, increase heat and cook until it just starts to simmer. Reduce heat to lowest setting and add mushrooms and beer. Cook for about 5-6 minutes more, stirring often.

Serves 4.

BEST VEGETARIAN CHILI

¾ lb.	dried pinto beans
¼ lb.	dried kidney beans
6 cups	chicken stock
¾ cup	Munich Helles lager
1	onion, diced
1 Tbsp	olive oil
1	red bell pepper, coarsely chopped
1	green bell pepper, coarsely chopped
1 Tbsp	serrano chili, diced
12 oz.	tomato paste
1	tomato, seeded, diced
2 Tbsp	chili powder
1 tsp	cayenne
1 Tbsp	paprika
½	orange
½ cup	coffee
1 Tbsp	unsweetened cocoa powder
	salt

Soak pinto and kidney beans in water overnight (or use quick-preparation instructions on package). Drain and rinse. Add chicken stock and beer to beans and simmer for 1½ hours or until beans are tender. Add additional chicken stock or water as necessary to keep beans covered with one inch of liquid while cooking. Meanwhile, in separate skillet, sauté onion in olive oil until soft. Add peppers and serrano chilies and cook 5 minutes, stirring often. Add tomato paste, tomato, chili powder, cayenne, paprika, juice of ½ orange, cocoa, and coffee; stir together, reduce heat, and simmer 15 minutes. Add simmered mixture to beans and cook 20-30 minutes longer. Add salt to taste.

Serves 6.

GREEN BOCK CHILI

2½ lbs.	boneless pork roast, cut into half-inch cubes
1 Tbsp	olive oil
1 lb.	pork soup bones
44 oz.	canned tomatoes, chopped
23 oz.	tomato sauce
1 Tbsp	garlic powder
1½ cups	bock beer
2 cups	water
21 oz.	diced green chilies (three 7 oz. cans)
2	jalapeno peppers, minced

Brown pork and soup bones in large pan. Remove and set aside. In large saucepan (5 quarts or larger), combine tomatoes, tomato sauce, garlic, beer, water, and cooked pork and bones. Boil for 20 minutes. Add jalapenos and green chilies and boil another 20 minutes. Reduce heat and continue cooking to desired thickness. Remove bones and serve.

Serves 8

FRENCH ONION SOUP

2 lbs.	white onions, sliced
4 Tbsp	butter
2 Tbsp	flour
1 cup	Scotch ale
5 cups	beef stock
1 tsp	salt
½ tsp	black pepper
6 slices	French bread
8 oz.	Swiss or gruyere cheese, grated

Sauté onions in butter until golden. Add flour and stir for about 1 minute. Slowly add beer and beef stock; cover and bring to a boil. Reduce heat and simmer 15-20 minutes. Add salt and pepper. Ladle soup into 6 oven-proof bowls or tureens. Sprinkle grated cheese on each bread slice and place a bread slice in each bowl. Heat in 400° oven for about 5 minutes or until cheese melts. Serve immediately.

Serves 6.

SCOTCH ALE VICHYSSOISE

6	small leeks, sliced (white part only)
2	onions, chopped
8 Tbsp	butter (1 stick)
1¼ lbs.	yellow potatoes (not baking potatoes), peeled and diced
1 cup	celery, chopped
1 tsp	salt
1 tsp	black pepper
5 cups	chicken stock
1 cup	Scotch ale
2 cups	cream

Sauté onions and leeks in butter until translucent. Add potatoes, celery, salt, pepper, and chicken stock and cook until potatoes are tender, about 45 minutes. Run mixture through food processor or blender until smooth; chill. Just before serving, stir in Scotch ale and cream.

Serves 8.

COUNTRYSIDE BEAN SOUP

1 cup	dry pinto beans
½ lb.	cooked ham, cubed
2 cups	water
2 cups	chicken stock
1½ cups	tomato juice
1	small onion, chopped
1 clove	garlic, minced
1 Tbsp	fresh parsley, chopped
2 Tbsp	brown sugar
½ tsp	salt
⅛ tsp	ground cloves
1	bay leaf
¼ tsp	celery seed
½ tsp	tarragon
¼ cup	bitter

Wash beans and soak overnight in enough water to cover. Drain and rinse well. Combine all ingredients except beer in pot (at least 4-quart). Bring to a boil, reduce heat and simmer, covered, until beans are tender, about 3 hours. Remove 4 cups of soup, cool, and blend in food processor or blender. Return to pot, heat to serving temperature, stir in beer and serve.

Serves 4.

ITALIANO SOUP

2 cans	garbanzo beans (15½ oz. cans)
4 slices	bacon
1 clove	garlic, minced
1 cup	carrots, sliced
¾ cup	onions, chopped
1 cup	celery, chopped
12 oz. can	tomatoes, chopped
3½ cups	chicken broth
½ tsp	black pepper
⅛ tsp	rosemary, ground
2 Tbsp	fresh parsley, chopped
½ cup	export lager

Drain chickpeas and puree in food processor with 1 cup of chicken stock. Cook bacon in large skillet, drain, cool and break into pieces; set aside. In the skillet with bacon grease, sauté garlic, carrots, onions, and celery about 5 minutes. Add all ingredients to a large pot and bring to a boil. Reduce heat to a simmer and cook 15 minutes, stirring occasionally.

Serves 4.

VEGETABLE BEER SOUP

1 cup	celery, chopped
1 cup	carrots, diced
1 cup	onion, diced
1 Tbsp	butter
6 cups	chicken stock
1 cup	cheddar cheese, grated
½ tsp	mustard, dry
⅛ tsp	liquid hot pepper sauce
⅛ tsp	Worcestershire sauce
½ tsp	salt
½ tsp	black pepper
1½ cups	Pilsener

Sauté celery, carrots, and onions in butter until just starting to brown. Bring stock to a boil in separate pot, add vegetables and simmer for 45 minutes. Add cheese to soup, stirring constantly until cheese is melted. Stir in spices and beer; serve immediately.

Serves 6.

THICK AND CHEESY VEGETABLE SOUP

½ cup	carrots, diced
½ cup	celery, diced
2	onions, diced
2	potatoes, large, diced
1½ cups	pale ale
1½ cups	water
1 Tbsp	instant chicken bouillon
3 cups	cheddar cheese, shredded
1 cup	milk
1 tsp	salt
¼ tsp	cayenne
⅛ tsp	nutmeg

In large saucepan, combine carrots, celery, onions, potatoes, beer, water, and chicken bouillon; bring to a boil. Reduce heat and simmer, covered, until vegetables are tender, about 20 minutes. Remove about half the vegetables, cool slightly, and puree in blender. Return the vegetable puree to the pan along with the remainder of the ingredients. Stir over low heat until cheese melts; do not boil. Serve immediately.

Serves 6.

JUST CHEESE SOUP

¾ cup	onions, minced
3 cloves	garlic, minced
6 Tbsp	butter
6 Tbsp	flour
1½ cups	pale ale
3 cups	chicken stock
½ lb.	cheddar cheese, grated
¾ cup	cream
1 tsp	salt
½ tsp	black pepper

Sauté onions and garlic in melted butter in heavy pan until onions are translucent, about 5-6 minutes. Whisk in flour two tablespoons at a time until blended. Slowly whisk in chicken stock and ale. Bring to a boil, stirring constantly; reduce heat and simmer about 6 minutes. Add cheese slowly, stirring until well blended. Stir in cream and heat to serving temperature; do not boil. Season with salt and pepper and serve.

Serves 6.

ROASTED GARLIC SOUP

12	large garlic cloves, unpeeled
4	large onions, chopped
3 Tbsp	olive oil
6 cups	chicken broth
1 cup	Munich Helles
1 tsp	thyme
1	medium potato, peeled and diced
1 tsp	salt
½ tsp	black pepper

Roast garlic cloves (whole) in a 325° oven for about 30 minutes or until soft. Cool. Squeeze garlic from skins and mash the pulp; discard skins. In a large heavy saucepan or Dutch oven, sauté onions in olive oil until translucent. Add mashed garlic, broth, beer, and thyme; bring to a boil. Reduce heat and simmer about 15 minutes. Add the potato and simmer another 15-20 minutes until potato chunks are tender. Cool the mixture slightly and puree in a food processor. Return to a saucepan, add salt and pepper and heat to serving temperature.

Serves 6.

FISH STEW

6 Tbsp	olive oil
4	onions, sliced
1	red bell pepper, sliced
1	green bell pepper, sliced
½ lb.	mushrooms, sliced
⅛ tsp	thyme
¼ tsp	salt
¼ tsp	pepper
2 cups	water
32 oz.	canned tomatoes, with juice
1½ cups	cream ale
4 lbs.	whitefish fillets, skin removed and cut into bite-size chunks
¼ cup	fresh parsley, chopped

In large saucepan, sauté onions in oil until translucent. Add the peppers and cook about 5 minutes, stirring often. Add mushrooms, thyme, salt, pepper, water, and tomatoes with their juice; bring to a boil. Reduce heat and simmer 15 minutes. Add the beer and fish and continue to cook until the fish flakes easily, about 15 minutes. Stir in parsley and serve.

Serves 8.

KAREN'S SPECIAL

2	large ham hocks, smoked
7 cups	water
1 cup	doppelbock
28 oz. can	tomatoes, diced, with juice
3 cans	hominy (15 oz. cans). drained
1	large onion, chopped
2 tsp	salt
1 tsp	pepper
1 tsp	sugar
1 lb.	cooked pork, shredded or diced (can be from the hocks)
1	lime, cut into 6 slices
6 Tbsp	sour cream

In large pot, simmer hocks uncovered in water for 2 hours. Add all remaining ingredients except lime and sour cream; bring to a boil, reduce heat and simmer 30 minutes. Remove the hocks and serve with a slice of lime and tablespoon of sour cream on top of each bowl.

Serves 6.

Main Dishes

HAM 'N SWISS ON RYE CASSEROLE

10 oz.	rye bread, cut in cubes
3 cups	green apples, chopped
1 cup	red onion, chopped
16 oz.	sauerkraut, drained and rinsed
¼ cup	Dijon mustard
¼ cup	mayonnaise
½ cup	rye ale or pale ale
2½ cups	Swiss cheese, grated
½ lb.	deli ham, sliced and chopped

Bake bread cubes in 400° oven until crisp, about 10 minutes. Put half of the bread into a shallow 3 quart baking dish. In a separate bowl, combine apples, onion, sauerkraut, mustard, mayonnaise, ham, and half the cheese. Combine this mixture with the bread in the baking dish, stirring lightly. Pour the beer evenly over the dish. Cover with foil and bake at 350° for about 50 minutes. Uncover, spread the rest of the bread over the mixture, sprinkle remainder of cheese over that and bake until cheese is browned, about 20 minutes.

Serves 4-6.

GREEN CHILI CASSEROLE

1½ lbs.	chuck roast, boneless, trimmed
1 Tbsp	olive oil
8 oz.	green chilies, diced
1 can	tomatoes, diced (14 oz. can)
1 can	black beans (15 oz. can)
1 can	cream of chicken soup (10¾ oz. can)
1 cup	quick cooking brown rice
¼ cup	Pilsener
2 Tbsp	salsa
1 tsp	cumin
½ cup	cheddar cheese, grated

Cut beef into 1" x 2" strips. Brown meat in small batches in hot skillet with oil; drain meat and set aside. Combine all remaining ingredients except cheese in a skillet or large pan; bring to a boil. Add meat and pour into a 2-2½ quart casserole dish and bake at 375° uncovered for 25 minutes or until rice is cooked. Sprinkle with cheese and bake 2-3 minutes longer.

Serves 6.

BODACIOUS FRITTATA

4 strips	bacon
¾ cup	yellow onion, diced
¾ cup	celery root, diced
¾ cup	parsnip, diced
¾ cup	carrots, diced
1 cup	Napa cabbage, shredded
6	eggs
¼ cup	stout
1 tsp	salt
1 tsp	basil
1 tsp	black pepper
½ tsp	garlic powder
¼ tsp	celery seed
1½ cups	cheddar cheese, grated

Fry bacon in 10-inch, oven-proof skillet (preferably cast-iron). Remove bacon when crisp, drain on paper towel, crumble bacon when cool, and set aside. Remove all but one tablespoon of bacon grease from skillet. Sauté all vegetables except cabbage in bacon grease in skillet until just tender, stirring frequently. Add cabbage and cook one more minute. Beat eggs in mixing bowl with beer, seasonings, and reserved bacon pieces. Pour egg mixture over vegetables in pan, stir together and cook until just set. Sprinkle with cheese and place under broiler until cheese starts to brown, about 2 minutes.

Serves 4.

MARINATED PAPRIKA PORK CHOPS

6	¾" thick pork loin chops
1½ cups	export lager
1	onion, sliced
3 Tbsp	butter
1	bay leaf
½ tsp	thyme
2 tsp	paprika
¾ tsp	lemon juice
¼ tsp	garlic powder
½ tsp	dry mustard
½ tsp	sage
½ tsp	basil
¼ tsp	salt
¼ tsp	black pepper
1 cup	mushrooms, sliced

Marinate pork chops in beer overnight in the refrigerator. Reserve marinade and pat pork chops dry. Melt butter in heavy skillet (large enough to hold all pork chops in single layer) and brown the pork chops on each side; remove pork chops. Sauté onions in pan until translucent. Add one cup of marinade to onions in skillet with remaining ingredients. Bring to a boil and add pork chops in single layer. Reduce heat to low and simmer, covered, for 20 minutes. Remove bay leaf and serve with liquid and mushrooms spooned over pork chops.

Serves 6.

CORNED BEEF AND CABBAGE

5	onions
2 lbs.	carrots
5-6 lbs.	corned beef, brisket or round
½ cup	cider vinegar
1 cup	stout (not sweet or oatmeal)
1 Tbsp	mustard seed
1 Tbsp	coriander seed
½ Tbsp	black peppercorns
½ Tbsp	whole allspice
2	bay leaves
½ Tbsp	dill seed
3 lbs.	cabbage

Dice 1 cup carrots and 1 cup onions. Place in the bottom of large kettle or pan (at least 12 quarts). Set corned beef on top and add liquid from corned beef packet. Add vinegar, stout, spices, and enough water to barely cover meat. Bring to a boil. Reduce heat, cover, and simmer for 2-3 hours, until meat is fork-tender. Cut remainder of onions into wedges and cut carrots into 1-2 inch chunks. Cut each cabbage into 8 wedges. Add carrots and onions, then cabbage wedges to simmering meat. Cover and continue simmering until cabbage wedges are done (25-35 minutes). Remove vegetables and keep warm. Remove meat, let stand for 15 minutes and slice across grain. Serve with vegetables.

Serves 10-12.

GLAZED BAR-BEER-QUE CHICKEN

4	chicken breasts, boneless, skinless
¼ cup	soy sauce
½ cup	wheat beer
¼ cup	fresh squeezed orange juice
1 cup	honey
2 cloves	garlic, minced
1 Tbsp	fresh ginger, minced

Combine all ingredients except chicken in a glass bowl. Add chicken and marinate in refrigerator overnight. Grill chicken over medium coals or in broiler, basting with marinade every few minutes. Cook until chicken is just done, about 15 minutes, turning once.

Serves 4.

CHICKEN MANDALAY

1	onion, chopped
4 cloves	garlic, minced
1 Tbsp	fresh ginger, minced
2 Tbsp	olive oil
1½ cups	coconut milk
1 tsp	salt
1 tsp	cumin
1 tsp	coriander
1	jalapeno, minced
4	chicken breasts, boneless, skinless
1 cup	alt beer
2 Tbsp	lime juice
2	green onions, chopped
¼ cup	fresh cilantro, chopped
½ cup	roasted peanuts, chopped

In a heavy skillet, sauté onion, garlic, and ginger in 1 tablespoon olive oil until onion is translucent. Remove mixture, let cool, and place in blender with coconut milk, salt, cumin, coriander, and jalapeno; blend until smooth. Add 1 more tablespoon oil to skillet and sauté chicken breasts on each side until lightly browned. Pour coconut milk mixture and beer over chicken. Simmer at low heat uncovered about 25 minutes. Remove chicken and keep warm in serving dish. Add lime juice, cilantro, and green onions to skillet, stirring until bubbly. Pour sauce over chicken, sprinkle chopped peanuts on top and serve.

Serves 4.

COUNTRY CLUB CHICKEN

1 cup	Pilsener
¼ cup	olive oil
1 Tbsp	lemon juice
1 clove	garlic, mashed
1½ tsp	basil
½ tsp	rosemary
4	chicken breasts, skinless, boneless
4 slices	deli ham, thinly sliced
4 slices	provolone or gruyere cheese, about 2 inches by 1 inch each
½ cup	buttermilk
½ cup	parmesan cheese, grated
2 Tbsp	parsley, minced

Cut deep pocket in the large side of each breast. Combine beer, olive oil, lemon juice, garlic, basil, and rosemary. Marinate chicken in beer mixture in refrigerator for 4 hours. Pat chicken breasts dry and stuff each with one ham slice wrapped around a cheese slice. Combine parmesan and parsley. Dip chicken in buttermilk and dredge in parmesan mixture. Place in baking dish and bake at 375° for 25 minutes or until juices run clear.

Serves 4.

ROAST PORK

6 lbs.	boneless pork roast, rolled and tied
6 cloves	garlic, split
1½ cups	porter
¼ cup	olive oil
2 Tbsp	butter, melted
1 Tbsp	basil
2 tsp	marjoram
1½ tsp	black pepper
1½ tsp	salt
1 tsp	sage
1 tsp	rosemary

Cut slits in pork roast every few inches and stuff with split garlic pieces. Combine remaining ingredients and pour over pork roast in rectangular baking pan. Cover and refrigerate overnight, turning occasionally. Drain and reserve marinade. Roast pork (fat side up) in preheated 325° oven until meat thermometer registers 160°-165°, about 3 hours. Baste frequently during last half hour with marinade. Let stand for 15-20 minutes before carving.

Serves 8.

CHICKEN AND RICE PILAF

1 cup	white rice, uncooked
1 cup	Pilsener
¼ cup	water
½ envelope	dry onion soup mix
1 can	cream of mushroom soup (10¾ oz. can)
2 Tbsp	pimientos, diced or chopped
4	chicken breasts, boneless, skinless
1 tsp	paprika
½ tsp	salt
½ tsp	pepper

Mix rice, beer, water, onion soup mix, pimientos, and mushroom soup together in an 8" x 11" glass baking dish. Place chicken breasts on top of mixture and sprinkle the salt, paprika and pepper over the breasts. Bake uncovered at 375° for 60 minutes or until chicken and rice are tender.

Serves 4.

ORANGE BAKED CHICKEN

1	chicken, about 2½ lbs., cut into serving pieces
¾ cup	French dressing, bottled
1 cup	honey beer
½ cup	orange juice
1 tsp	cornstarch

Marinate chicken pieces in French dressing for at least one hour, stirring lightly to coat. Place chicken in oven-proof dish under broiler for several minutes until browned. In saucepan, heat beer, orange juice, and cornstarch together until slightly thickened. Pour over chicken. Bake chicken at 375° for 60 minutes, basting occasionally with pan juices.

Serves 4.

INSIDE-OUT CHICKEN AND STUFFING

12 oz.	herb seasoned stuffing mix
2 Tbsp	butter, melted
1¼ cups	chicken broth
3 cups	chicken, cooked, diced
¾ cup	bitter
¾ cup	onion, diced
½ cup	celery, diced
½ cup	mayonnaise
½ tsp	salt
2	eggs
1½ cups	milk
1 can	cream of mushroom soup (10¾ oz. can)
½ cup	cheddar cheese, grated

Mix together stuffing, butter, and chicken broth. In separate bowl, combine chicken, beer, onion, celery, mayonnaise, and salt. Spread half of the stuffing in a greased casserole dish (at least 13" x 9"). Spread the chicken mixture over the stuffing and then cover with the remaining stuffing. Whisk together the eggs, milk, and soup and pour evenly over the stuffing. Bake covered at 325° for 30 minutes. Sprinkle with cheese and continue to bake, uncovered, for 5 minutes more.

Serves 8.

HUNGARIAN GOULASH

1 Tbsp	olive oil
2 lbs.	round steak, cut into one-inch cubes
2	onions, coarsely chopped
5 Tbsp	flour
2 cups	beef broth
2 Tbsp	paprika
1 tsp	cumin
1 Tbsp	vinegar
1 cup	cream ale
¾ cup	sour cream

Heat oil in heavy pot or Dutch oven. Brown meat in oil, remove meat and set aside. Add onions to pot and sprinkle with 2 tablespoons flour, stirring until onions are lightly browned. In separate bowl, stir 3 tablespoons of flour into 1 cup of the beef broth until smooth. Add the broth/flour mixture to the pot, along with spices, vinegar, beer, remainder of broth, and meat. Cover and simmer until meat is tender, about 2 hours. Add more broth as necessary to keep meat covered with liquid. Stir in sour cream and serve in a bowl over noodles.

Serves 6.

MUSHROOM AND SCALLOP PASTRIES

1 Tbsp	butter
½ lb.	mushrooms, sliced
1 lb.	scallops, small
¼ cup	Belgian ale
4 oz.	cream cheese
12 sheets	phyllo dough
	Cooking spray

Melt butter over moderate heat in a skillet that has a lid. Add mushrooms and cook several minutes until mushrooms start to soften. Add scallops and ale, cover, and cook five minutes. Reduce heat, add cream cheese, and stir until cheese is just melted. Remove from heat and let cool slightly to handle. On three sheets of the phyllo dough, place ¼ of the mixture about one inch from the far edge of the sheets. Keep remaining sheets covered with a damp cloth. Roll the dough towards you over the mixture, folding in the sides after rolling about halfway. Continue rolling and pinch the seam to seal. Place the completed pastry seam side down in a lightly greased baking pan. Repeat for the remaining pastries. Spray each pastry quickly with cooking spray and bake at 400° for 20-25 minutes until golden.

Serves 4.

SPAGHETTI AND BEER SAUCE

24 oz.	tomato sauce
18 oz.	tomato paste
½ cup	dark lager
½ tsp	sugar
1 stalk	celery
2	bay leaves
⅓ cup	Parmesan cheese, grated
1 lb.	spaghetti

Combine all ingredients except spaghetti in large saucepan. Bring to a boil, reduce heat, then simmer for at least 1 hour, stirring occasionally. Remove celery stalk and bay leaves. Cook spaghetti according to package instructions. Serve sauce over spaghetti.

Serves 8.

OVEN-BARBECUED FISH

1 Tbsp	olive oil
4 cloves	garlic, minced
2	onions, diced
2 cups	tomato sauce
1½ cups	bock beer
¼ cup	brown sugar
2 Tbsp	cider vinegar
1½ Tbsp	soy sauce
2 tsp	fresh ginger, minced
1 Tbsp	Worcestershire sauce
½ tsp	cayenne
2 tsp	liquid smoke
2½-3 lbs.	firm fish fillets (such as trout, red snapper, tuna)

In a 2-quart saucepan, sauté onions and garlic in olive oil until onion is translucent. Add the remaining ingredients except liquid smoke and fish. Bring to a boil, then reduce heat and simmer 30 minutes, stirring occasionally. Stir in the liquid smoke. Place fish in shallow greased baking pan and bake at 450° for 5 minutes. Pour sauce liberally over fish and continue cooking, 10 minutes for each inch of thickness. Baste occasionally with additional sauce to ensure fish does not dry out. Serve immediately.

Serves 6.

SMOKED BEER PORK CHOPS

8	pork loin chops
1	onion, diced
3 cloves	garlic, minced
15 oz.	tomato sauce
1½ cups	rauchbier
2 Tbsp	vinegar
4 Tbsp	Worcestershire sauce
¼ cup	butter
1 Tbsp	celery seed
1 tsp	dry mustard
1½ Tbsp	sugar
1 tsp	salt
1 tsp	black pepper
1 dash	liquid hot pepper seasoning

Combine all ingredients except pork chops in a 2 quart saucepan. Bring to a boil, reduce heat, and simmer 20 minutes, stirring frequently. Sear pork chops on grill, about 4 minutes on each side. Baste the chops liberally with sauce and return to grill. Over slow heat, cook chops 15-20 minutes or until done, turning every five minutes, basting with sauce before each turn.

Serves 4.

SLOW-GRILLED CHICKEN

2	chickens, cut into serving pieces
15 oz.	tomato sauce
2 cloves	garlic, minced
¼ cup	soy sauce
1½ cups	Munich Helles
¼ cup	cider vinegar
1 tsp	salt
2 tsp	red pepper flakes
1 tsp	black pepper

Place chicken skin side up in greased baking pan and bake at 450° for 45 minutes. Drain fat from pans. In a 2 quart saucepan, combine remaining ingredients, bring to a boil, lower heat and simmer 20 minutes, stirring occasionally. Pour sauce over chicken in pans and marinate at room temperature for 1 hour, basting frequently. Prepare a very slow fire on the grill and add wood chips soaked in water to create smoke. Place chicken on grill and cook for about 60 minutes, turning once.

Serves 6.

APPLE-NUT STUFFED PORK CHOPS

10 Tbsp	butter, divided
½	onion, chopped
⅓ cup	walnuts, chopped
½	apple, chopped
8 oz. pkg	herb seasoned dry stuffing mix
1 cup	brown ale
6	pork chops, double rib, 2" thick

In a large skillet, melt 8 tablespoons (1 stick) butter; add onions and cook until translucent, about 4-5 minutes. Remove from heat and stir in the apple, walnuts, stuffing mix and beer until well-mixed. Cut a slit about 1½" or 2" deep in the side of each pork chop. Fill each pocket with 1/6 of the stuffing mix. In the skillet, melt 2 tablespoons butter and brown the pork chops on each side, turning carefully so stuffing doesn't fall out. Place the chops on a baking pan in a preheated 350° oven. Cover and bake 60-70 minutes until no longer pink at the center; meat thermometer should read at least 165°-170°.

Serves 6.

COQUILLES ST. JACQUES

2 Tbsp	onion, minced
6 Tbsp	butter
1 lb.	scallops
1 Tbsp	lemon juice
½ tsp	salt
¼ tsp	marjoram
¾ cup	steam beer
¼ lb.	mushrooms, sliced
¼ cup	flour
1 cup	cream
1 Tbsp	fresh parsley, minced
½ cup	bread crumbs

In medium saucepan, cook onion in 1 tablespoon butter until onion is translucent. Add scallops, lemon juice, salt, marjoram, beer, and mushrooms. Simmer uncovered for 10 minutes; set aside. In another saucepan, melt 5 tablespoons butter over low heat, then whisk in the flour until smooth. Remove from heat and stir in scallop mixture, cream, and parsley. Divide mixture into 6 individual shells or place entire mixture in a shallow casserole. Sprinkle bread crumbs over the top and broil for 5-8 minutes, until bubbly and just browned.

Serves 6.

SOUR CREAM LAMB CHOPS

8	shoulder lamb chops
2 cloves	garlic, split
2 Tbsp	olive oil
1½ cups	sour cream
1½ Tbsp	Worcestershire sauce
1 tsp	black pepper
1 tsp	salt
½ tsp	paprika
¼ cup	cream ale
2	bay leaves

Rub cut garlic cloves over the lamb chops. In a heavy skillet, heat the olive oil and brown the chops on both sides. Remove the lamb chops and place them flat in a large casserole dish. To the pan drippings in the skillet, add all the remaining ingredients except the bay leaves. Cook over medium heat for 2 minutes, stirring well to combine. Pour the mixture over the lamb chops, place bay leaves on top, and bake at 350° for 50-60 minutes.

Serves 4.

HOMETOWN BEEF AND CHEESE CASSEROLE

6 oz.	egg noodles, uncooked
4 oz.	cream cheese
½ cup	green onions, chopped
2 Tbsp	parsley, chopped
¾ lb.	ground chuck
2 Tbsp	vegetable oil
1	onion, chopped
½ cup	celery, chopped
1 clove	garlic, minced
½ Tbsp	salt
1 tsp	black pepper
½ tsp	thyme
1 tsp	oregano
½ tsp	dry mustard
1 tsp	garlic powder
1 cup	brown ale
4 oz.	tomato sauce
1½ cups	Monterey Jack cheese, grated

Cook noodles according to package directions; rinse, drain, and set aside. Combine cream cheese, green onions, and parsley in a bowl and set aside. In a large heavy skillet, brown the beef, drain well, and set meat aside. Heat vegetable oil in the skillet over medium heat for several minutes. Add onions, celery, garlic, and seasonings. Stir constantly until onions are translucent, about 6 minutes. Stir in the beer, tomato sauce, and meat. Bring to a boil, remove from heat and stir in the cream cheese mixture until well blended. Place half the noodles in a casserole dish, cover with half of the meat mixture and ½ cup Monterey Jack cheese, then cover with the rest of the noodles, meat mixture and cheese. Ensure there is some sauce on all exposed noodles or they will become hard and crispy in the oven. Bake uncovered at 350° for about 20 minutes until cheese is browned and bubbly.

Serves 4.

SALMON BRECKENRIDGE

2 lbs.	canned red salmon, boned and flaked
2	eggs
1 cup	milk
1 cup	Pilsener
1 cup	potato chips, crushed
2 Tbsp	butter, melted
⅓ cup	onion, minced
1 tsp	dill
½ tsp	tarragon

Drain salmon and pick over to remove bones or skin. Combine all ingredients and mix well. Place in greased 2-quart casserole and bake at 400° for 45 minutes.

Serves 4.

HAM AND POTATO CASSEROLE

1 Tbsp	olive oil
2	onions, chopped
10 oz. pkg	frozen spinach, thawed, chopped
3 Tbsp	butter
3 Tbsp	flour
1¾ cups	milk
2	eggs, beaten
2 cups	cheddar cheese, grated
¼ cup	bock beer
1 Tbsp	mustard
½ tsp	pepper
1 lb.	ham, fully cooked, cubed
24 oz. pkg	frozen shredded hash browns, thawed

In large skillet, cook onions in olive oil until translucent. Drain spinach well and combine with onions; set aside. Melt butter in saucepan and stir in flour. Add milk to saucepan and continue to cook until milk starts to simmer. Remove from heat. Temper the eggs by adding ½ cup of the hot milk mixture to the beaten eggs and stir briefly; return the egg/milk combination to the saucepan. Stir in 1½ cups cheese, beer, mustard, and pepper. Place half of the ham cubes in a casserole dish (at least 2 quart capacity). Spread half of the drained hash browns over the ham and half the cheese mixture over the hash browns. Spread all the spinach/onion mixture over the sauce, then layer the remaining ham, hash browns, and cheese sauce. Sprinkle the reserved ½ cup grated cheddar over the top. Bake at 350° uncovered for about 30 minutes.

Serves 6.

BEEF STROGANOFF

2 lbs.	boneless beef tenderloin or sirloin
¾ cup	flour
½ Tbsp	salt
¼ tsp	pepper
6 Tbsp	butter, divided
1	small onion, chopped
1 lb.	mushrooms, sliced
2 cans	beef broth, undiluted (10¾ oz. cans)
1¼ cups	honey beer
1 cup	sour cream
3 Tbsp	tomato paste
1 tsp	Worcestershire sauce

Cut meat into 2" x ½" x ¼" strips. Dredge meat strips in mixture of flour, salt, and pepper. Brown meat on all sides in large skillet with 3 tablespoons butter. Set meat aside. Melt the remaining 3 tablespoons butter in a skillet and sauté onions and mushrooms over medium heat for about 5 minutes. Add meat, broth and beer to the skillet, cover and simmer 20 minutes. Remove from heat and blend in sour cream, tomato paste, and Worcestershire sauce. Serve over egg noodles, pasta, or rice.

Serves 4.

PAPRIKA CHICKEN

3-4 lbs.	chicken, assorted pieces, skin removed
3 Tbsp	olive oil
3	onions, chopped
1 Tbsp	salt
1 tsp	black pepper
1 tsp	onion powder
1 tsp	basil
½ tsp	thyme
3 cloves	garlic, minced
¼ cup	paprika
6 oz.	tomato paste
2 cups	chicken stock
1½ cups	amber lager
1 cup	sour cream

Heat oil in large Dutch oven (about five quart size), and brown chicken on all sides. Set chicken aside. Add onions, seasonings, garlic, and paprika, stirring constantly and scraping bottom of pot often. Cook until onion starts to brown, about five minutes. Stir in tomato paste, stock, and beer; bring to a boil. Return the browned chicken to the Dutch oven. Bring back to a boil, reduce heat, cover and simmer about 30 minutes. Remove from heat and stir in the sour cream until completely blended. Serve immediately over noodles or rice.

Serves 6.

ALICE'S GUMBO

1 lb.	andouille sausage
7 cups	chicken stock
1½ cups	Pilsener
¾ cup	vegetable oil
¾ cup	flour
2	onions, chopped
2	green bell pepper, chopped
1 cup	celery, chopped
⅓ cup	fresh parsley, chopped
1 Tbsp	salt
2 tsp	paprika
½ tsp	onion powder
½ tsp	cumin
2 tsp	black pepper
1 tsp	dry mustard
1½ tsp	thyme
1½ tsp	garlic powder
3	bay leaves
3 lbs.	chicken, breasts and thighs, skin removed

Cut andouille sausage into slices about ½ inch thick and fry in a heavy skillet or Dutch oven until browned. Remove and drain the sausage. In a heavy 8-quart stockpot, heat chicken stock and beer, bringing it to a boil as the roux and vegetables are being prepared. For the roux, heat vegetable oil in the skillet or Dutch oven until hot. Test by dropping in a pinch of flour; if it sizzles quickly the temperature is right (if it turns black the oil is too hot; if it just floats, the oil is too cool). Add the flour in two parts, whisking constantly until the flour is blended with the oil. When all the flour has been added, continue cooking and whisking until the roux is a light chocolate color. Add the chopped onions, peppers, and celery to the roux, continuing to stir for about 5 minutes. Add the bay leaves and the seasonings, stirring often to ensure nothing burns. After about 10 minutes, add the roux/vegetable mixture a cup at a time to the boiling chicken stock, whisking to ensure the roux is smoothly blended in the stock. Add the chicken and browned sausage to the stock and vegetables, bring to a boil, then reduce heat and simmer for about 30 minutes, until chicken is done (thighs may take longer—test with a fork to ensure juices run clear). Remove chicken and allow the pieces to cool enough to handle. Leave the stockpot at a simmer. Remove chicken meat from bones and shred. Return the chicken and any accumulated juices to the stockpot and serve.

Serves 8

SHRIMP CREOLE

½ cup	flour
½ cup	vegetable oil
1 clove	garlic, minced
1 cup	onion, chopped
½ cup	celery, chopped
½ cup	green bell pepper, chopped
15 oz.	tomato sauce
3 oz.	tomato paste
2½ cups	water
½ cup	brown ale
1½ tsp	salt
⅛ tsp	cayenne
¼ tsp	black pepper
1½ lbs.	medium shrimp, peeled
1 Tbsp	fresh parsley, chopped
2 Tbsp	green onion, chopped

Heat oil in heavy pan or Dutch oven to make roux. When oil is hot, add flour ¼ cup at a time, whisking constantly to ensure flour is absorbed. Continue cooking until roux is medium brown. Add garlic, onion, celery, and bell pepper and cook until soft. Add tomato paste and tomato sauce and cook another 5 minutes, stirring often. Stir in water, beer, salt, cayenne, and black pepper; simmer 1 hour. Add shrimp and cook another 10 minutes. Just before serving, stir in parsley and green onion. Serve over white rice.

Serves 8.

PALE ALE POT ROAST

3 Tbsp	olive oil
4 lbs.	boneless round or rump roast
3	onions, chopped
1	green bell pepper, chopped
1	red bell pepper, chopped
3 cloves	garlic, minced
¾ cup	pale ale
2	medium tomatoes, chopped (with juices)
1 Tbsp	salt
2 tsp	thyme
2 tsp	rosemary
1 tsp	marjoram
1 tsp	sage
10	green olives, pitted and sliced
½ cup	fresh parsley, chopped

Dry the beef thoroughly and brown on all sides in olive oil in a large heavy pot or Dutch oven (with cover). Remove the roast and, in the same pot, sauté onions, peppers, and garlic for about 5 minutes. Add the meat, beer, tomatoes, and seasonings; cover and cook slowly over low heat for 2½-3 hours or until cooked to desired point. Remove meat and let stand for 10-15 minutes before slicing. Meanwhile, increase temperature under sauce and continue to cook until sauce thickens. Stir olives and parsley into the sauce and serve over sliced meat.

Serves 6-8.

SCOTCH ALE, SAUSAGE, AND CABBAGE CASSEROLE

16-18	large cabbage leaves (from 1 large head)
1 lb.	bulk pork sausage
¼ cup	Scotch ale
½ cup	fresh parsley, chopped
4 cloves	garlic, minced
½ tsp	black pepper
½ tsp	nutmeg
3	eggs, beaten
	cooking spray

Cook cabbage leaves in boiling salted water until barely tender, about 5 minutes. Remove leaves intact, cool, and pat dry. Combine remaining ingredients in mixing bowl. Cover the bottom of a Dutch oven with 5-6 cabbage leaves. Spread half of the sausage mixture over the cabbage, add another layer of 5-6 cabbage leaves and spread the remainder of the sausage mixture over that. Place the remaining cabbage leaves over the top of the sausage layer. Spray the top of the casserole with cooking spray. Bake uncovered at 350° for about 1¾ hours, ensuring pork is completely cooked. Check periodically during last half hour and spray top again with cooking spray if cabbage is starting to scorch. Cool for 10-15 minutes. Cut into wedges for serving.

Serves 6.

BAKED FISH WITH
PILSENER/LIME SAUCE

4	firm white fish fillets
½ cup	canned chicken broth
¼ cup	Pilsener
1 Tbsp	cornstarch
¼ cup	lime juice

Bake fish at 400° until just barely done, about 10-12 minutes for ½" fillets. While fish is baking, bring chicken broth to a boil in sauce pan. In a separate bowl, whisk cornstarch and beer together until smooth. Whisk beer/cornstarch mixture into broth and return to boil. Continue whisking and add lime juice. Stir constantly for about 1 minute, until mixture thickens. Place fish fillets on serving platter, spoon sauce over fish and serve.

Serves 4.

HONEY MUSTARD AND BOCK CHOPS

3 Tbsp	olive oil
4 Tbsp	honey
⅓ cup	Dijon mustard
½ cup	bock beer
2 tsp	rosemary, dried and crushed
4 cloves	garlic, minced
4	pork loin chops
2 Tbsp	butter
⅓ cup	cream

Combine oil, honey, mustard, bock, rosemary, and garlic in glass bowl. Add pork chops and marinate in refrigerator for at least one hour, turning occasionally to coat. Remove chops and reserve marinade. Melt butter in heavy skillet (large enough to hold all pork chops in single layer) and brown the pork chops on each side. Cover, reduce heat to low and continue to cook until just done; remove chops and keep warm on serving platter. Add marinade to skillet, bring to a boil, remove from heat and stir in cream. Serve immediately over pork chops.

Serves 4.

BEER BRAISED BEEF

1½ lbs.	round steak
2 Tbsp	flour
1 Tbsp	vegetable oil
1½ cups	Munich Helles

Pat steak dry; sprinkle all over on both sides with flour. Heat oil in large heavy skillet with lid; skillet must be large enough to hold the steak when placed flat in pan. When oil is hot, brown the round steak, about 3-4 minutes each side. Add beer, cover, and simmer about two hours, until beef is tender. Add additional water or beer to keep some liquid in skillet while cooking. When done, let rest for 15 minutes. Serve meat in large pieces, or shred with a fork and serve on rolls with barbecue sauce, such as Sizzling Sauce (see Sauces, Salsas and Dressings).

Serves 4.

ROSEMARY THIGHS

2 Tbsp	olive oil
2 Tbsp	butter
2 cloves	garlic, crushed
12	chicken thighs, skin removed
1 large sprig	fresh rosemary
¼ tsp	salt
¼ tsp	black pepper
1½ cup	alt beer

Heat oil and butter in large heavy pan with a lid. Add garlic and cook over low heat until golden brown; remove garlic. Add chicken in one layer and brown on all sides over medium high heat. Add rosemary, salt, pepper, and beer. Bring to a boil, reduce heat and simmer, covered, until chicken is done (juices run clear when pierced), about 30-40 minutes. Place chicken on serving platter. Skim fat from pan juice and pour juices over the chicken.

Serves 4.

TEMPTING FATE

2 lbs.	ground beef, shaped into 4 patties
4	bratwurst
2 cups	Pilsener
¼ lb.	butter (one stick)

Simmer bratwurst in water for 30 minutes to pre-cook. Melt butter with beer in a heavy pan (with a lid) large enough to hold the meats. Grill hamburgers and bratwurst over medium coals until done. Place meats in beer/butter mixture and simmer covered for up to 30 minutes. Serve meat on buns with condiments.

Serves 4.

Light Rye Bread, Cornbread, and Cherry Kriek Bread

Bodacious Frittata

Glazed Bar-Beer-Que Chicken, Barleywine Coleslaw, and Potatoes, Peppers and Pilsener

83

Smoked Beer Pork Chops

Spaghetti and Beer Sauce, Marinated Mushrooms, and Salad with Beer Vinaigrette Dressing

85

Rosemary Thighs

Imperial Cranberry Stout Salsa, Cheese Dip, and Salsa Cerveza

Porter Steamed Clams with Sheepherder's Bread

CRISPY FISH FILLETS

¼ cup	amber lager
⅓ cup	flour
1	egg white
¼ tsp	salt
¾ cup	bread crumbs
1 oz.	nuts, finely chopped (peanuts, pecans, or Brazil nuts)
¼ tsp	black pepper
1 lb.	fish fillets, cut into serving size pieces

Whisk together beer, flour, egg white and salt. In separate bowl, combine bread crumbs, nuts, and pepper. Place a greased rack on a baking sheet. Dip fish pieces in bread crumbs, then in egg/beer mixture, then in bread crumbs to coat well, and place on the rack. Bake in a preheated 450° oven for 10-15 minutes, until golden brown and fish is opaque in the middle and flakes easily.

Serves 4.

CARBONNADE

2	onions, coarsely chopped
3 cloves	garlic, minced
½ tsp	thyme
2 Tbsp	olive oil
½ lb.	mushrooms, sliced
1 cup	flour
2 lbs.	beef, cubed
2 tsp	wine vinegar
3 cups	export lager
½ cup	beef stock
1	small leek, washed well and trimmed
1	bay leaf
1 tsp	brown sugar
½ tsp	salt
¼ tsp	black pepper

In large skillet, sauté onions, garlic, and thyme in 1 tablespoon olive oil until onion is translucent, about 5 minutes. Add mushrooms to the skillet and sprinkle 2 tablespoons flour over all; stir to coat. Remove the onions, garlic, and mushrooms to a 5-quart Dutch oven or stew pot. Dust meat cubes with remaining flour. Heat 1 tablespoon oil in the skillet and brown meat cubes on all sides, being careful not to crowd them. Add meat to Dutch oven, along with wine vinegar, beer, beef stock, leek, and bay leaf. Stir to mix and simmer, covered, for about 2 hours, until meat is tender. Remove and discard leek and bay leaf; add brown sugar, salt and pepper. Serve over noodles, rice, or potatoes.

Serves 4.

BRAZILIAN CHICKEN

6 Tbsp	olive oil
¾ cup	wheat beer
¼ cup	parsley, chopped
	juice of 1 lemon
1	onion, chopped
1 tsp	savory
1 tsp	coriander
4	mint leaves, bruised
¼ tsp	garlic powder
1 tsp	salt
¼ tsp	black pepper
1	large frying chicken, cut into serving pieces, skinned
1 Tbsp	butter
½ cup	tomato sauce
1 cup	water
1 Tbsp	cornstarch

Combine first eleven ingredients in glass or ceramic bowl. Add chicken and marinate overnight in refrigerator, turning chicken once. Remove chicken pieces and reserve marinade. In heavy pot or Dutch oven with a lid, brown the chicken pieces in butter. Add tomato sauce and ½ cup water to the marinade and pour the mixture over the chicken. Cover and simmer until chicken is tender and juices run clear, about 1 hour. Remove chicken to serving platter. Stir cornstarch into ½ cup cold water until smooth. Bring pot liquid to a boil, add cornstarch solution, continue to cook until desired thickness, then pour over chicken.

Serves 4.

WILD WHITE HOUSE CHICKEN

1 can	cream of celery soup (10¾ oz. can)
1 can	cream of chicken soup (10¾ oz. can)
½ envelope	dry onion soup mix
¾ cup	India Pale Ale
¼ cup	water
1 cup	wild rice
6	chicken breasts, boneless, skinless

Combine soups, dry mix, beer, water, and rice in wide casserole dish with a cover; let stand several hours. Place chicken breasts on top of mixture. Cover and bake at 350° for 1½ hours. Uncover, stir gently and continue to bake until moisture is absorbed and rice is tender, about ½ hour more.

Serves 6.

Side Dishes

DILLED CARROTS

4	large carrots, peeled, julienned
1 Tbsp	butter
2 tsp	dill
1 cup	Christmas beer
¼ tsp	salt
1 tsp	sugar

Sauté carrots in butter over medium heat until lightly browned. Add beer and dill, cover, and simmer for 15 minutes, stirring often. Add salt and sugar; cook uncovered another 3-4 minutes.

Serves 4.

BEER BATTERED VEGETABLES

¾ cup	corn starch
¼ cup	flour
1 tsp	baking powder
½ tsp	salt
¼ tsp	pepper
¼ tsp	garlic powder
¼ tsp	basil
⅓ cup	porter
1	egg, lightly beaten
½ lb.	broccoli
¼ lb.	cauliflower
¼ lb.	carrots
1 cup	vegetable oil

For batter, combine dry ingredients, then stir in beer and egg. Pat vegetables dry and cut into serving size chunks. Heat oil in wok, deep fryer, or skillet until hot, 375°. Dip vegetable pieces in batter, then fry a few at a time in the oil; remove when golden brown and drain on paper towels.

Serves 4.

MUSHROOM PILAF

8 Tbsp	butter (1 stick)
1½ cups	uncooked rice
1 can	condensed onion soup (10½ oz.)
½ can	condensed beef consomme (10½ oz. size can)
¾ cup	alt beer
½ lb.	mushrooms, sliced thickly

Melt butter in 2-3 quart casserole dish. Add rice and stir to coat well. Add remaining ingredients and stir to combine. Cover and bake at 325° for 1 hour or until rice is tender. Stir occasionally and add water if mixture becomes dry.

Serves 6.

CUBAN BLACK BEANS AND RICE

3 cans	black beans (16 oz. cans), undrained
1	green pepper, coarsely chopped
1	onion, diced
1	jalapeno, minced
1 clove	garlic, minced
2 tsp	vinegar
½ cup	brown ale
1	bay leaf
2 tsp	oregano
¼ tsp	liquid hot pepper seasoning
5 oz. pkg	saffron or yellow rice

Combine all ingredients except rice in a large saucepan. Bring to a boil, reduce heat and simmer about 1 hour, stirring occasionally. Cook rice according to package instructions. Serve beans over rice.

Serves 6.

GOLDEN VEGETABLES

1 lb.	broccoli
1 lb.	cauliflower
1 can	cheddar cheese soup (10¾ oz.)
¼ cup	Christmas beer
⅛ tsp	nutmeg
2 Tbsp	bread crumbs
4 slices	bacon

Cut broccoli and cauliflower into bite size pieces; steam until just tender. Spread broccoli and cauliflower in a shallow 1½ quart baking dish. Combine soup, beer, and nutmeg; pour over vegetables. Sprinkle bread crumbs over top. Bake at 350° for 20 min. Fry bacon until crisp, drain and crumble. Spread bacon over cooked vegetables and serve.

Serves 6.

POTATOES, PEPPERS AND PILSENER

2 lbs.	potatoes (russet are best), peeled and sliced
1	red bell pepper, sliced thinly into circles
1	green bell pepper, sliced thinly into circles
½ cup	grated Parmesan cheese
2 tsp	thyme
1 tsp	salt
1 tsp	black pepper
2 Tbsp	olive oil
1 tsp	parsley
¼ cup	chicken broth
⅓ cup	Pilsener

Overlap ⅓ of the potato slices to cover the bottom of a 8" x 8" greased glass baking dish. Layer ½ of the red and green bell peppers over the potatoes. Sprinkle half of the cheese, thyme, salt, and pepper over the potatoes and peppers. Drizzle 1 tablespoon of olive oil over all. Add another layer of overlapping potatoes using another third of the slices, top with the remainder of the peppers, and sprinkle the remainder of the thyme, salt, and pepper over all. Drizzle with 1 tablespoon of olive oil. Make a final layer of potatoes with the remaining slices. Mix the beer and broth together and pour over the casserole. Sprinkle parsley and the remainder of the Parmesan cheese over the top. Cover and bake at 375° for 1 hour. Remove cover and bake another ½ hour until potatoes are tender and top is golden brown.

Serves 6.

RED BEANS AND RICE

¾ lb.	dried red beans
¼ lb.	dried kidney beans
3 cups	onions, chopped
1 cup	green bell pepper, chopped
½ cup	celery, chopped
1½ cups	pale ale
7 cups	chicken stock
2 tsp	salt
1½ tsp	onion powder
1½ tsp	dried basil
1 tsp	dry mustard
1 tsp	black pepper
½ tsp	oregano
6 cups	white rice, cooked

Soak beans overnight in enough water to cover by 3 inches. Drain and rinse beans. Sauté onions, green pepper and celery in heavy 5-quart stockpot, stirring constantly until vegetables start to soften. Add seasonings and continue to stir for 2-3 minutes. Add beer, chicken stock, and beans. Bring to a boil, then reduce heat and simmer for 1½ hours, or until beans are tender. Serve over rice.

Serves 6.

TANGY RED CABBAGE

6 cups	red cabbage, shredded (1 small head)
1	apple, peeled, cored, and diced
¼ cup	raisins
½ cup	water
¼ cup	sugar
3 Tbsp	cider vinegar
1 Tbsp	lemon juice
2 Tbsp	fruit beer
1 Tbsp	butter
½ tsp	salt
¼ tsp	pepper

In large covered skillet, cook cabbage, apple, and raisins in ½ cup water until cabbage is tender, about 10 minutes. In a small bowl , dissolve the sugar in the vinegar, lemon juice, and beer. Stir the liquid into the cabbage in the skillet along with the remainder of the ingredients. Simmer covered about 5 minutes, stirring occasionally.

Serves 6.

GREEN BEANS AND BROWN ALE

1	large onion, chopped
3 Tbsp	olive oil
¾ cup	green pepper, diced
½ cup	celery, diced
1 lb.	green beans, French cut, frozen
¼ cup	Brown Ale
¼ cup	water

Sauté onions in olive oil in large frying pan until translucent. Add green pepper and celery and cook over moderate heat for 5-6 minutes. Thaw green beans and drain. Add beans, ale, and water to vegetables and simmer covered for 20 minutes, stirring occasionally.

Serves 6.

BEER MUSTARD BEETS

2 tsp	prepared mustard
1 Tbsp	Imperial stout
3 Tbsp	butter, softened
4	beets, medium, peeled and diced

Combine mustard, stout, and butter. Cook beets in boiling water for about 10 minutes or until tender; drain. Put beets in serving dish while warm, dot with butter mixture, and toss lightly to coat.

Serves 4.

ZUCCHINI CHEESE CASSEROLE

3 cups	zucchini, grated
1 cup	cracker crumbs
1 cup	cheddar cheese, grated
2	eggs, beaten
¼ cup	doppelbock
2 Tbsp	onion, chopped
1 tsp	salt
½ tsp	pepper
1 dash	liquid hot pepper seasoning

Press and drain grated zucchini. Combine all ingredients well and put in buttered 8" x 8" casserole dish. Bake at 350° for 1 hour.

Serves 6.

EXTRAORDINARY BAKED BEANS

1 lb.	ground beef
½	green bell pepper, chopped
1	onion, chopped
2 cans	baked beans (16 oz. cans)
¼ lb.	mushrooms, chopped
¾ cup	catsup
¼ cup	barleywine
½ cup	maple syrup
1 tsp	salt

Sauté beef, green pepper, and onion together until beef is browned; drain. Combine all ingredients and bake in 9" x 13" casserole dish for 2 hours at 250°.

Serves 6-8.

HERBED YELLOW SQUASH

8	small yellow squash
3 Tbsp	butter
2	green onions, chopped
⅛ tsp	thyme
⅛ tsp	marjoram
⅛ tsp	rosemary
2 Tbsp	soy sauce
¼ cup	cream ale

Slice squash thinly. Sauté in butter until just barely limp, about 10 minutes. Add onions, thyme, marjoram, and rosemary and sauté another 2 minutes, stirring often. Add soy sauce and beer, stirring to coat well.

Serves 6.

DANISH LIMA BEANS

1 Tbsp	butter, melted
¼ cup	bread crumbs
10 oz. pkg	baby lima beans, frozen
2 Tbsp	milk
2 Tbsp	export beer
¼ cup	bleu cheese, crumbled

In small bowl, mix butter and bread crumbs; set aside. Cook lima beans according to package instructions and place in serving dish. In small saucepan, stir together beer, milk, and cheese over low heat until cheese is melted and combined. Pour over beans and top with bread crumbs.

Serves 4.

DELMONICO POTATOES

5	medium potatoes
2 Tbsp	butter
2 Tbsp	flour
1 cup	milk
¼ cup	Munich Helles
½ tsp	salt
¼ tsp	black pepper
3	hard-boiled eggs, chopped
1 cup	cheddar cheese, grated
1 Tbsp	pimiento, chopped

Peel, slice and boil potatoes until just done. Melt butter in saucepan, whisk in flour, then pour in milk and beer and continue whisking until blended. Add salt and pepper and cook until thickened. In greased 2-quart casserole, spread the potatoes in the bottom, then a layer of eggs, then white sauce and sprinkle with cheese. Toss pimientos over the top and bake at 350° for 20 minutes.

Serves 6.

SPECIALTY POTATOES AND CHEESE

5 Tbsp	butter, divided
3 Tbsp	flour
½ tsp	salt
⅛ tsp	pepper
¾ cup	evaporated milk
¾ cup	Christmas beer
1 cup	cheddar cheese, grated
4 cups	potatoes, diced, cooked
½ cup	black olives, sliced
½ cup	soft bread crumbs

Melt 3 tablespoons butter in saucepan. Whisk in flour, salt, and pepper. Gradually stir in milk and beer and cook at medium heat, stirring constantly as mixture thickens. Add cheese and continue stirring until melted and smooth. Lightly toss potatoes and olives together in 2 quart casserole dish. Pour cheese sauce over the top. Melt the remaining 2 tablespoons butter and mix with bread crumbs; sprinkle over casserole. Bake at 350° for 30 minutes.

Serves 6.

STUFFED ONIONS

6	large onions
4 Tbsp	butter, divided
½ cup	green bell pepper, chopped
¼ cup	celery, chopped
2 cups	mushrooms, chopped
½ cup	chopped nuts (Brazil nuts, filberts, walnuts, or pecans)
½ lb.	ground beef
2 cloves	garlic, minced
2 tsp	salt
2 tsp	black pepper
1½ tsp	thyme
1½ tsp	basil
1 tsp	garlic powder
2 cups	provolone cheese, grated
½ cup	porter
1½ cups	chicken stock

Bake unpeeled onions in a baking pan for 35 minutes at 350°. Remove from oven. When cool enough to handle, remove skins and slice off each end. Remove the inner onion layers, leaving about half-inch-thick onion bowls. Chop the inner layers of the onion and combine with the green pepper, celery, and 2 tablespoons butter in a skillet; sauté until vegetables are tender. Add the mushrooms and cook 2 minutes more. Remove to a mixing bowl. Toast the nuts for 3-4 minutes in a hot skillet; add to the vegetable mixture. Brown the ground beef with the garlic until meat is cooked; drain. Add the seasonings, stir and combine with the vegetable mixture. Set each onion on its flat bottom on a baking dish and stuff with the vegetable/meat mixture. Melt the other 2 Tbsp butter and combine with porter and chicken stock; pour over each onion. Bake the onions at 475° for about 10-12 minutes.

Serves 6.

BARLEYWINE COLESLAW

6 Tbsp	barleywine
1 Tbsp	butter
1 Tbsp	sugar
1 tsp	salt
½ tsp	black pepper
½ tsp	dry mustard
1	egg, slightly beaten
2 Tbsp	heavy cream
3 cups	cabbage, shredded

Combine barleywine, butter, sugar, salt, pepper, and mustard in saucepan; bring to a boil. Stir some of the hot liquid into a separate bowl with the egg, then return the egg/liquid mixture to the saucepan and stir to combine. Cook until it thickens and remove from heat; stir in the cream. While still hot, mix thoroughly with the cabbage. Chill before serving.

Serves 6.

Breads

DARK BEER RYE

2 packages	yeast
½ cup	warm water
2 Tbsp	butter, melted
¼ cup	molasses
1½ cups	dark lager beer (at room temperature)
2 tsp	salt
2 Tbsp	caraway seeds
3 cups	white flour
3 cups	rye flour

Sprinkle yeast over warm water in a large bowl; stir gently and let stand for 5-10 minutes. Mix together butter, molasses, beer, salt, and caraway seeds in separate bowl; stir into yeast/water mixture. Stir in two cups white flour until blended. Add rye flour and knead; add remainder of white flour as necessary to make elastic dough. Knead thoroughly. Cover with towel or cloth and let rise in a warm place until doubled in volume, about an hour. Punch down, divide in half and place in greased bread pans. Let rise again until doubled, about an hour. Bake at 350° for one hour or until crust is browned. Cool on rack.

Makes 2 loaves.

SHEEPHERDER'S BREAD

2 pkgs	yeast
2 cups	warm water (110°)
1 cup	Pilsener or pale lager (110°)
⅓ cup	sugar
2 tsp	salt
¼ lb.	butter, melted
8½ cups	flour

Sprinkle yeast over water, beer, and sugar in a large bowl; let stand about 5 minutes. Mix in salt, butter, and flour. Knead by hand, adding up to another cup of flour if necessary to make dough satin smooth and not sticky. Place in greased bowl and cover with hand towel; let rise in warm place until dough has doubled, about one hour. Meanwhile, liberally grease a 5-quart Dutch oven, including the lid. Punch down the dough, knead lightly and make a ball. Place dough in Dutch oven, cover with lid, and set in warm place to let dough rise again, about 30-40 minutes. Bake covered for 12 minutes in a 375° oven. Remove the lid and bake another 30-35 minutes. Remove loaf from Dutch oven and let cool on a rack.

Makes 1 large loaf.

LIGHT RYE

2 Tbsp	honey
1 Tbsp	butter
¾ cup	pale ale
2 pkgs	dry yeast
½ cup	warm water (110°)
2 tsp	salt
1 tsp	caraway seed
½ tsp	garlic powder
2½ cups	white flour
1¼ cup	rye flour

In small pan, heat the honey, butter, and beer until warm, about 110°. In large bowl, dissolve the yeast in warm water. Stir in the beer mixture, salt, caraway seed, and garlic powder. Combine the two flours in a separate bowl and add 1½ cups of the flour mixture to the liquid; mix until well combined. Stir in remaining flour, adding more white flour if necessary to make a soft dough. Knead for about five minutes and shape into a ball. Press the ball into a greased 8" round baking pan. Cover with a hand towel and let rise in a warm place for about 45 minutes. Bake at 375° for 30 minutes. Turn out of pan and cool on rack.

Makes 1 loaf.

DONNA'S GLAZED POPPY SEED BREAD

3 cups	flour
1½ tsp	baking powder
1½ tsp	salt
3	eggs
1 cup	milk
½ cup	fruit beer
2½	cups sugar
1 cup	vegetable oil
1½ Tbsp	poppy seeds
2 tsp	vanilla extract
2 tsp	almond extract

Combine ingredients in large bowl and beat with electric mixer for 2 minutes. Pour into two 5" x 9" loaf pans and bake at 350° for one hour. Remove from pan and cool. In a separate bowl, prepare glaze:

¾ cup	sugar
½ tsp	vanilla extract
½ tsp	almond extract
¼ cup	orange juice

Stir together until smooth and pour evenly over cooled bread.

Makes 2 loaves.

CHERRY KRIEK BREAD

2 cups	flour
1 cup	sugar
1 tsp	baking powder
½ tsp	salt
½ cup	shortening
¼ cup	Kriek (Lambic) Belgian ale
¼ cup	Maraschino cherry juice
2	eggs
½ tsp	vanilla extract
3 drops	almond extract
6 drops	red food coloring
8 oz.	Maraschino cherries, cut up
½ cup	nuts, chopped

Stir together all ingredients until thoroughly combined. Spoon into lightly greased and floured loaf pan. Bake at 350° for 1 hour. Cool on rack.

Makes 1 loaf.

CORNBREAD

1 cup	cornmeal
1 cup	white flour
4 tsp	baking powder
2 Tbsp	sugar
½ tsp	salt
1	egg
¼ cup	shortening, melted
½ cup	milk
½ cup	honey beer

Combine all ingredients in mixing bowl. Pour into a greased 8" x 8" baking pan. Bake at 400° for 30 minutes. Cool and cut into squares.

Makes 1 pan.

Sauces, Salsas, & Dressings

SALSA CERVEZA

1¼ lb.	tomatoes, seeded, drained and chopped (or 28 oz. can ready-cut tomatoes, drained)
¼ cup	Pilsener or chili beer
¼ cup	fresh cilantro, chopped
½ cup	onion, chopped
4	jalapenos, minced (use fewer if using chili beer)
1 clove	garlic, minced
½ tsp	salt
½ tsp	sugar

Combine all ingredients. Let stand for at least 2 hours; chill if desired.
Makes about 2½ cups.

DOPPELBOCK MUSTARD

6 Tbsp	dry mustard
5 Tbsp	white vinegar
5 Tbsp	doppelbock
6 Tbsp	butter
2 Tbsp	flour
5 Tbsp	sugar

In medium saucepan, combine mustard, vinegar, and beer; let stand 45 minutes. Cut butter into small chunks and add to mustard mixture with flour and sugar. Bring to a boil, stirring often. Remove from heat just as it starts to boil. Store in refrigerator or use warm. Especially good served with a selection of cooked sausages.

Makes about 1½ cups.

SIZZLING SAUCE

1 cup	ketchup
¼ cup	export lager
1 Tbsp	lemon juice
1 Tbsp	vinegar
¼ cup	molasses
2 cloves	garlic, pressed
3 Tbsp	onion, minced
2 tsp	chili powder
1½ tsp	black pepper
½ tsp	cayenne

Combine all ingredients in medium sauce pan and bring to a boil, stirring often. Reduce heat and simmer uncovered for 20 minutes. Serve over grilled ribs or beef brisket.

Makes about 1½ cups.

WHEAT BEER MAYONNAISE

3	egg yolks
3 Tbsp	wheat beer
1½ tsp	salt
1 Tbsp	Dijon mustard
1½ cups	oil (corn, canola, olive, or a combination of the three)

Have all ingredients at room temperature before starting. In a warm bowl, whisk together the egg yolks, beer, salt and mustard until slightly thickened. While continuing to whisk, add the oil, drop by drop. As the mayonnaise begins to thicken, add the oil faster, continuing to whisk until the desired consistency is reached. Finally, whisk in one teaspoon of very hot water. Refrigerate for at least 2 hours before using.

Makes about 1¾ cups.

SEAFOOD SALSA

2	medium tomatoes, seeded, chopped
¼ cup	onion, chopped
½ cup	fresh cilantro, chopped
2	medium jalapeno peppers, chopped
¾ tsp	cumin
1 tsp	sugar
1 tsp	salt
1 Tbsp	lime juice
¼ cup	amber lager

Combine all ingredients in a food processor and pulse until chunky. Serve over grilled or baked fish.

Makes about 1½ cups.

IMPERIAL CRANBERRY STOUT SALSA

	Zest of 1 orange (reserve juice)
¾ cup	water
2 Tbsp	fresh ginger, minced
⅝ cup	sugar (½ cup and 2 Tbsp)
12 oz.	fresh cranberries
	Juice of 2 limes
½ cup	cilantro, chopped
3	jalapenos, minced
2 Tbsp	Imperial stout

Peel zest off orange and mince. Combine with water, ginger, and ½ cup sugar in saucepan. Heat slowly until it forms a thick syrup. Finely chop cranberries in food processor. Combine cranberries, syrup, orange juice, lime juice, the remaining sugar and the other ingredients in a bowl. Chill until ready to serve.

Makes about 3 cups.

SOUTH AMERICAN STEAK SAUCE

¼ cup	wheat beer
½ cup	extra virgin olive oil
1 Tbsp	oregano
1 cup	fresh parsley, minced
3 cloves	garlic, minced
¼ tsp	crushed red pepper
¼ tsp	salt

Combine all ingredients and serve. Especially good with grilled steaks.
Makes about 1 cup.

BERRY GOOD SALSA

2 cups	raspberries, rinsed and drained
1	Bartlett pear, peeled and diced
4	large prunes, diced
¼ cup	Framboise Belgian ale
¼ tsp	black pepper

Combine ingredients, stirring gently. Chill. Serve over grilled chicken.
Makes about 3 cups.

PIQUANT BBQ SAUCE

¾ cup	fruit beer
½ cup	molasses
¼ cup	lemon juice
¼ cup	orange juice
1 Tbsp	dry mustard
3 cloves	garlic, minced
½ tsp	cinnamon
½ tsp	allspice

Combine all ingredients in a small saucepan. Bring just to a boil, stirring often.
Remove from heat. Serve with pork ribs or grilled chicken.

Makes about 1¾ cups.

CHEESE SAUCE

3 Tbsp	butter
3 Tbsp	flour
½ cup	milk
½ cup	alt beer
¼ tsp	salt
⅛ tsp	black pepper
¼ tsp	dry mustard
¾ cup	cheddar cheese, cubed

Melt butter in heavy saucepan. Whisk in flour until smooth; remove from heat. Add milk and beer; return to heat and bring to a boil for one minute, stirring constantly. Reduce heat to low and add remaining ingredients. Continue to stir and cook until cheese is melted and sauce is desired consistency, about 6-8 minutes. Excellent over steamed vegetables.

Makes about 1½ cups.

BEER VINAIGRETTE SALAD DRESSING

⅓ cup	pale ale
1 Tbsp	Dijon mustard
¼ tsp	salt
⅛ tsp	black pepper
½ cup	oil (vegetable or olive)

In small bowl, whisk together ale, mustard, salt, and pepper. Add the oil slowly, whisking constantly, until entire mixture is emulsified. Serve over green salad or vegetables.

Makes about ¾ cup.

BROWN ALE SAUCE

3 Tbsp	butter
1 Tbsp	onion, minced
3 Tbsp	flour
1½ cups	brown ale
2 tsp	beef bouillon granules
1½ tsp	Worcestershire sauce

Melt butter in sauce pan over low heat and sauté onion until light brown. Whisk in flour until smooth. Slowly add beer and other ingredients, stirring constantly until desired consistency is reached. Serve over beef or mashed potatoes.

Makes about 1¾ cups.

Entertaining with Beer

You can create a memorable social event by combining a beer-tasting with a beer dinner. To the disappointment of some die-hard beer fans, a "beer dinner" is not a meal consisting solely of beer; it is a menu including foods which are cooked with beer as an ingredient. The beer is not only the beverage for the evening but is a dinner ingredient and the entertainment as well. This is a particularly effective setting for a mixer with people who were previously unacquainted. Beer-tasters must mingle as they move about to sample from the different bottles and there is ample opportunity to strike up a conversation about the beers and their variety of flavors.

This section provides guidelines for planning, organizing, and executing a beer-tasting, including everything from beer theme ideas to recommended serving temperatures and sequences. For those who truly want to enjoy the beer, a section on the proper method for tasting is included. The beer dinner section provides a few tips on combining beers and food and contains sample menus for your evening, ranging from casual to formal.

127

Beer-Tasting Necessities

To have a successful beer-tasting session, you need only three ingredients: people, beer, and glasses.

PEOPLE

While it is possible to hold a beer-tasting with only one person, it loses some of the "party" aspects. You should have enough guests to ensure a diversity of opinions and not so many that you have to spend your evening washing the glasses. Eight to twelve is probably a manageable number. If the beer-tasting is part of a beer-cookery dinner, you certainly want to take into account your cooking skills, equipment, serving/eating area, and budget. The most important attribute of your beer-tasting cohorts is that they arrive with open minds (and open mouths). This is a night to expand everyone's gustatorial horizons.

BEER

You have several options for selecting and acquiring the beer for your tasting. The beer choices should be based on the beer knowledge and preferences of you and your guests:

For a group of people who have not yet been exposed to the variety of beer styles, you might want to pick a sampling from among the entire spectrum of beers available. For example, you could have a Pilsener, doppelbock, India Pale Ale, brown ale, porter, stout, barleywine, and wheat beer.

If you want to narrow the choices somewhat, you could focus on a particular family of beers, such as lagers or ales. An ale-tasting evening could include a brown ale, bitter, pale ale, Lambic, porter, and Imperial stout.

Another way to restrict the field of selections is to taste the beers from a particular country or region of the world. For example, the beers of Australia, East Asia, Belgium, Canada, or Scandinavia would make a fine beer-tasting evening. If you choose this option, be sure there is sufficient variety in beers from that area—a tasting of "beers from Namibia" would most likely be short and uninspiring.

If your guests are somewhat familiar with general beer styles and tasting methods, they may enjoy examining the particular aspects and brewery variants of a single beer style, such as Pilsener, stout, Belgian ale, or wheat beer. Your tasting will sample the skills of various brewers of that single style of beer. This will require access to enough different brands of the selected style to ensure a good mix of tasting selections. As part of your planning process, make sure that enough are available locally.

✺ Many brewers create special beers around the Christmas season. These brews can be the basis for a party, sampling the different holiday specialty beers.

✺ The truly creative party planner can assemble beers by any other criteria they wish (e.g., green bottles only, twist-off caps, brand names that begin with "F", breweries with free tours). Keep in mind that these more whimsical offerings make it difficult to do any serious comparison by beer style. But, it's your party!

There are various options available to you for acquiring the beer for your party. You can: (1) buy the beers yourself; (2) have a general "pot-luck"; or (3) make purchasing assignments to the guests. If you buy the beer yourself, you have the most control, but also incur a potentially significant expense. If you try the potluck approach, be sure that you narrow the choices somewhat for each guest to ensure adequate variety (i.e., tell one to "bring a porter" and another to "arrive with your favorite Pilsener", etc.) While this method reduces expenses and pre-party trips to the store, you should advise guests of the proper temperature for their style. You do not want to delay your tasting as you wait for an Imperial stout that arrived ice cold to warm to an appropriate serving temperature. If your guests are suitably cooperative, your least expensive and most efficient option for acquiring beers is simply to tell each guest what to bring, by brand name and style. Appendix C lists some examples of brand names available in the U.S. and the styles they represent.

How much beer should you have? It depends on how many different beers you will be tasting and how many people are invited. Six to ten different beer styles is probably enough for an evening, since your sensory perceptions will start to blur with repeated tastings and the taste buds will slowly become desensitized from the alcohol. Each person should be able to try a 1 or 2 ounce serving of each separate beer type for adequate tasting. And some will probably want to try it again, because they didn't notice a flavor or aroma that someone else did. At a minimum, allow 3 or 4 ounces of each different beer per person for tasting. For example, if you are inviting six people to a tasting, plan to have two 12 oz. bottles of each beer available. It is important not to have too many different beers available at a beer tasting—guests typically feel compelled to sample all of them and could become quite intoxicated despite the small sample sizes.

Do not stop your beer quantity calculation here, though. It is unlikely that the guests will be satisfied with just tasting the beer; they will probably want some of their favorites to quaff as they compare post-tasting notes. Plan to have an additional one or two bottles per person of the more popular styles available after the tasting. While it is difficult to determine in advance what will be "popular," experience has shown that the heavier beers (Imperial stouts, doppelbocks) and very distinctive beers (rauchbier, Belgian ales) are not as likely to be selected as the beverage of choice by folks accustomed to American Pilsener. When in doubt, pick extras of what you like—at least you know someone will drink it. If you are serving dinner following the beer-tasting, have a bottle or two per person of the styles that best accompany your menu (see the suggestions in Chapter Five).

With a few quick calculations you can see that a beer-tasting with six people and eight different beers to sample necessitates about sixteen bottles of beer (4 ounces per person, per beer style). Your calculations should always be tempered with your knowledge of individual alcohol tolerances and the situation. The goal is to enjoy the myriad variation of tastes in beer, not to become intoxicated. Be a responsible host/hostess.

GLASSES

The most important characteristic of a beer glass is cleanliness. Residue from the cleaning process, such as soap, detergent, oil, or grease, will destroy the subtle character of a beer. A dirty glass will not hold a proper head, either. To get a glass properly cleaned for beer tasting, wash it well, rinse thoroughly in hot water and allow it to air-dry. If you do not have enough glasses, plastic cups can be a last resort for your tasting, and certainly make the clean-up easier. Make sure to choose a hard smooth plastic with no odor. Beer bubbles should not adhere to the surface of a good plastic cup.

How many glasses do you need? If you want to rinse glasses after every beer sample, you only need one acceptable glass per person. This is not as bad as it sounds; you can provide a pitcher of fresh water and a waste water tub so each guest can swish out their own glass before moving on to different beers. If you have enough glasses that you can have several for each person, you might consider taking a break in the beer tasting to run them through the dishwasher, but make sure that they are air-dried, not toweled. Suitable plastic cups may be your best option if you have a limited amount of glassware and lots of friends.

Brewing up a Great Beer-Tasting

With the planning complete and the party hour approaching, it is time to get down to the actual drinking. Here are some considerations that will make the beer-tasting more enjoyable and best demonstrate the beer styles represented.

HANDLING

Beer is a perishable and fragile product. Old age can contribute to off-flavors, but mishandling beer can also ruin a perfectly good brew. Beer is best when it is continuously refrigerated from brewery to serving glass. Keep the beer out of the light; a photochemical reaction can occur when beer is exposed to strong light, resulting in a skunky odor. This is the reason most beer bottles are brown or green—these colors are intended to neutralize the wavelengths that most affect beer chemistry. Some breweries using clear bottles chemically treat the hops (containing the primary light-susceptible element) to prevent adverse reaction to light. You should buy bottled beer from stores that keep it away from the light and preferably under refrigeration. Beer should not be agitated any more than necessary from the store to your refrigerator, since shaking increases the carbon dioxide pressure in the bottle and can lead to chemical reactions that are detrimental to flavor and aroma. Store your beer upright in a cool, dark place until consumed.

TEMPERATURE

It is important to serve beer at the proper temperature for the style. Lower temperatures tend to numb the palate and decrease your ability to detect the more subtle flavors crafted into the beer. Cold temperatures also prevent some of the delectable aromas from being released when you swirl the beer in your glass. Serve the beer at the temperature the brewery recommends, often noted on the label. In the absence of that information, serve lagers between 35 and 50 degrees and ales between 50 and 70 degrees, which are the approximate fermentation temperatures for these beer families. Serve Pilseners at the low end of the lager range and fuller-bodied lagers (e.g., bock, European dark) towards the upper end (45-50). Pale ales deserve the low end of the ale spectrum while the darker ales (porter, stout) should be offered above 55 degrees. Wheat beers are best served around 50-55 degrees, but 45 is acceptable on particularly warm days. Hybrid beers vary widely, but 45-50 degrees is probably a good rule of thumb.

TIME

How long should your beer-tasting last? Plan on at least ten minutes per different type of beer. This allows time for any palate-cleansing, glass rinsing, pouring, repeated sampling, and comparing erudite observations. If you are following the beer-tasting with dinner, add a few extra minutes to your time estimate for moving around and transferring glasses. If you will just be socializing and sampling favorites after the tasting, allow additional time as you would for any other successful party.

BEER IDENTIFICATION

You can hold an open tasting or a blind tasting. With an open tasting, the beer bottle labels are clearly visible as people pour their tasting sample. While this is the simplest method to execute, some people will have preconceived notions about the beer which could influence their observations about its flavor. With a blind tasting, a single beer is sampled and judged without the guests knowing the brand or style. This can be done by pouring all the samples in another room and bringing them out together, or by covering the labels at the serving table. Both of these blind tasting methods are somewhat cumbersome. Unless you are truly attempting to hone beer judging skills (or show an obnoxious individual that he or she doesn't know anything about good beer), there is nothing wrong with an open beer-tasting.

TASTING SEQUENCE

In order to ensure that the palate is not overwhelmed and desensitized to further tasting, it is important to taste the beers starting with those that are lighter and then moving towards the heavier and darker ones. To prove the validity of this tasting sequence, try a sip of a light Pilsener lager, then an Imperial stout, then the Pilsener again. No matter how tasty the Pilsener was before, it will now seem somewhat washed out as a result of the Imperial stout sampling. Here is a suggestion for the approximate order of beer tasting, from first to last:

Cream Ale • Wheat Beer • Pilsener • Belgian Ales • Export

Brown Ale • Bitter • Pale Ale • India Pale Ale • Munich Helles

Amber • Steam Beer • Alt • Dark Lager • Bock • Scotch Ale • Porter

Stout • Doppelbock • Imperial Stout • Barleywine

FOOD WITH BEER-TASTING

What should you serve to eat during the beer-tasting? The purpose of having food at this point in the evening is not to create a wonderful beer/food taste combination, but to cleanse the palate and have something in the stomach to avoid rapid intoxication. Whatever you serve, it should not overpower the beer flavors or interfere with the tasting sensors. Avoid greasy or salty foods completely. Loaves of French or Italian bread, salt-free crackers or pretzels, water crackers, rice cakes, plain bagels, or flat-bread are all good beer-tasting accompaniments and provide an absorbent beer cushion in the stomach.

JUDGING

If you would like to document your observations and opinions on the beer, you might want to have some judging forms available for people to use. A list of the terms typically used in judging is available in Appendix A and a sample beer judging form is shown in Appendix B. Remember, there isn't a right and wrong when it comes to what people like. There are some beers which are more representative of their style than others, but there is no good or bad beer style. *Viva la difference!*

How to Taste Beer

Enjoying a beer is a full sensory experience. To really appreciate the brewmaster's art, taste your beer as if you were a beer judge. You and your guests certainly do not have to follow a rigorous competitive outline for beer tasting. However, as you become more sensitive to the different beers available today, a critical approach will allow you to recognize variations and truly appreciate greatness when you find it. Additionally, it's fun to have a basis for comparison and a common language with your friends at the beer-tasting as you sip your way through the many styles. Here are some of the guidelines of beer judging that will make your beer sampling a more rewarding experience.

Use the correct glass, as discussed in the previous section, and proper pouring technique. First, look through the bottom of the bottle to see if there is sediment. Sediment is not necessarily bad. Many breweries now complete the fermentation in the bottle, called "bottle-conditioning," leaving a little yeast sediment on the bottom. Pour carefully, stopping before the sediment trail reaches the lip of the bottle. Obviously, you should only pour once, since returning the bottle to an upright position will mix the yeast sediment with the remainder of the beer again. Pour the beer into the glass in such a way as to produce about three-fourths to one inch of head. Depending on carbonation level, some beers may need to be poured straight down the center of the glass from high above while others may require only a careful trickle down the side to coax out the head.

SIGHT

Look at the beer's color. The hue is determined by the types of grain used to make the beer and the time and temperature of the wort boil. Dark, long-roasted grains produce a dark beer; lightly toasted grains give a more transparent, light-colored brew. A dark beer is not necessarily stronger than a lighter beer; color and alcohol content are not related. Take a look at the clearness, or clarity, of the beer. While it is not a significant part of the flavor profile, it will help you to distinguish among beer types. Finally, view the head on the beer. Small, enduring bubbles indicate natural carbonation while large inconsistent bubbles suggest carbon dioxide injection.

SMELL

Time to get even closer to the beer. Hold the glass under your nose and take two or three sharp whiffs. You will be able to detect the results of the brewer's hops selections in the flowery aroma. Other scents you may detect are the clean, sweet smell of roasted barley, yeasty aromas in bottle-conditioned brews, or esters lending a fruity smell. Unpleasant smells such as skunkiness, sulfur, or cardboard indicate mishandling of the beer.

TASTE

Finally! Down the hatch! But slowly. Take a good sip and roll it around in your mouth. The four taste areas on the tongue from tip to back are: sweet (tip of the tongue); salt (on the sides behind the tip); sour (on the sides toward the back); and bitter (across the back of the tongue closest to the throat). With that first mouthful, you will taste the sweetness of the malt on the tip of your tongue and the bitterness of the hops on the back. This malt-hop "balance" varies significantly between beer brands and styles—the malt sweetness dominates in some beers while others are definitely hoppy. This hop flavor may bear little resemblance to the hops aroma you detected as you smelled the beer. Hops can be used for different purposes: hops added during the boiling of the wort will impart flavor (bitterness) while hops added near the end of the brewing process (finishing hops) provide aromas. Savor the distinctions. Ain't beer wonderful?

FEEL

With another sip of beer rolling around in your mouth, feel the beer. Mouthfeel sensations can be light (watery), full (a sense of thickness or body), astringent, or warming. By the way, unlike our wine-sipping counterparts, beer tasters don't intentionally spit it out after tasting.

SUMMARY

Beer judges will also have a category for overall impression or drinkability (see Appendix B), which combines all elements of the sensory process. Unless you are handing out medals or trying to become a serious beer judge, you can just say "I like it" or "I don't like it." More creative party-planners can add some tailor-made terminology of their own to the Summary section of the judging form. For example, a best-to-worst rating system for your party could be:

1 – Would rather have a six-pack of this beer than a Hawaiian vacation.
2 – We should have had this beer at the wedding reception.
3 – I'm still glad you invited me, but I would like to sample another.
4 – "Bill" (any recognized, jerky-and-pickled-egg-eating acquaintance of the group) buys this beer.
5 – If I was wandering the Sahara and found a bottle of this beer, I'd chew sand.

Planning the Beer Dinner

A successful beer dinner requires not only some cooking skill and an appreciative guest list, but a bit of planning. You need to tailor the party to your personal situation and preferences by considering serving style, food combinations, presentation, and the party setting.

Menu Planning

First, consider the type of evening you are planning and who you are inviting. Will your dinner lean towards the more formal, or is it a blue jeans and T-shirt affair? How many people do you plan to invite? Then think about your serving capability. Do you have enough matching place settings or will you have to be less formal and use disposable or "variable-style" (unmatched) dishes? Look at your floor plan, chairs, tables and other potential eating surfaces. Where could that many people eat at the same time? Examining these questions will help you establish a serving style and decide how many different foods (or courses) to serve and where to eat. You probably will find that your facilities are incompatible with certain serving styles and party numbers. That's normal—just don't create an awkward situation for you and your guests by trying to force a particular style or party size into an inappropriate environment. This is supposed to be fun.

Anticipate the pathway you will use to get the food from the kitchen to the guests' mouths. The three basic serving methods typically used for parties are buffet style, family style, or formal.

Buffet style dinner service is the most casual and typically requires the least involvement by the host or hostess during the meal. The food is placed in a common area (table, counter, sideboard or whatever) and the guests serve themselves as they pass by the food. An area should be designated for eating and should have all the utensils and napkins already there if not available at the serving area.

≈ Family (English style) dinner requires a preset table for everyone, with the food already in serving dishes. Guests are all seated at serving time and the host or hostess individually fills each plate, which is then passed to the guest. A modification of this is to pass the serving dishes around the table for everyone to serve themselves.

≈ Formal, or Russian style, service is the most labor-intensive for the host and hostess, unless they hire or borrow assistance. Food is arranged on individual plates in the kitchen and placed before each guest at the table. This is repeated for each course.

It is possible, and often desirable, to combine these methods in your party service. For example, the salad could be prearranged on plates which are already on the table when the guests are seated. The subsequent courses could be passed around family style and afterwards the guests might retire to another room to serve themselves buffet-style from a dessert selection. Mix and match to suit your individual situation.

A casual dinner buffet need not have more than a few items, while a more formal dinner typically has a soup or salad, bread, main course, and dessert. The menu suggestions in this section are not intricate multi-course meals. Having a few items properly prepared and served is ultimately more impressive and enjoyable than a double-digit string of mediocre courses served by an over-stressed host or hostess.

Having decided upon a serving style, dining area, and number of foods or courses, you can start determining the individual recipes for your party menu. Deciding what to eat is almost as much fun as the eating itself. It may be necessary to put down napkins to avoid drooling damage as you look over the recipes. Sometimes the serving style selected will eliminate a few food choices; don't serve a meal that requires extensive knife-and-fork wizardry if you are eating from lap trays. Conversely, a buffet served from the grill quickly suggests certain foods and accompaniments.

Basic menu planning principles recommend that you try to use a variety of colors, flavors, temperatures, seasonings, cooking techniques, and textures. Offer contrasts between and within each course or menu selection. A heavy rich soup should not be followed by a main course with a cream sauce; a deep-fried appetizer should not precede a pan-fried main dish. All brown foods on a plate is boring. Follow rich foods with light, plain foods, offer simply prepared meats with an elaborate sauce, or serve something pureed with a crisp food. Avoid repetition.

The purpose of having a beer dinner is to recognize and appreciate the difference beer can make in cooking. For this reason, it is more advisable to make food selections that spotlight several different beer styles in the meal rather than just using one type of beer.

When you plan the beer dinner menu, make sure that you also consider your cookware and serving dishes. Think about which pot or pan will be required to prepare each dish. Write down an approximate sequence of events in the preparation process so you don't need one cooking item for two different dishes at the same time. A written sequence of preparation events will also avoid the ugly situation where you need the oven to be set at 325° and "broil" simultaneously. Make a list of which serving bowls/plates/platters will contain each menu item—don't forget to be equally specific about serving utensils. Avoid putting yourself into a position where you need to wash something while entertaining.

Also, if you plan a dinner which includes an outdoor grilled item (a wonderful party idea), consider the additional time and logistics of preparing the grill, transferring the food to and from the grill, keeping food warm while doing any other preparations, and any special handling utensils you may need, such as tongs, basting brush, spatula.

Dinner Menu Suggestions

Here are some menu ideas that correspond well to various kinds of dinner serving methods. Of course, you can use a buffet style menu suggestion as a formal dinner and vice-versa; these are just suggestions. Not all the foods listed here have a corresponding recipe in this cookbook; for foods such as rice, potatoes, green salad, or vegetables, you can just use basic cooking instructions or your own favorite version. A page number after a menu item indicates where to find the recipe in this book.

BUFFET

Beer-Battered Oysters[21]

Shrimp Creole[73] and Rice

Green Beans and Brown Ale[101]

Lemon Meringue Pie

Glazed Bar-Beer-Que Chicken[50]

Potatoes, Peppers and Pilsener[98]

Barleywine Coleslaw[110]

Brownies

Beddar Cheddar Spread[30] with crackers

Scotch Ale, Sausage, and Cabbage Casserole[75]

Dark Beer Rye Bread[111]

Oatmeal Raisin Cookies

Salsa Cerveza[117] with tortilla chips

Refried Bean Soup[31]

Green Chili Casserole[46]

Raw Vegetables (carrots, celery, jicama)

Flan

Hummus[18] with chips, crackers

Chicken Mandalay[51]

Baked Sweet Potatoes

Beer-Battered Vegetables[94]

Key Lime Pie

FAMILY

Cheese Sticks[29]

Green Salad or Relish Tray

Oven-Barbecued Fish[60]

Zucchini-Cheese Casserole[103]

Angel Food Cake

IPA Cheese Ball[22] with crackers

Countryside Bean Soup[37]

Inside-Out Chicken and Stuffing[56]

Herbed Yellow Squash[105]

Almond Cookies

Vegetable Beer Soup[39]
Tomato Slices and Dressing
Country Club Chicken[52]
Spinach Noodles or Pasta
Pecan Pie

Porter Steamed Clams[25]
Salmon Breckenridge[67]
Danish Lima Beans[106]
Sheepherder's Bread[112]
Fruit and Cheese Tray

Marinated Mushrooms[20]
Green Salad with Beer
Vinaigrette Dressing[126]
Italian Bread with garlic butter
Spaghetti and Beer Sauce[59]
Biscotti

Cheese Dip[24] and raw vegetables
Corned Beef and Cabbage[49]
Boiled or Mashed Potatoes
Soda Bread
Fruit Tarts

FORMAL

French Onion Soup[35]
Pale Ale Pot Roast[74]
Baked Potatoes
Golden Vegetables[97]
Ice Cream

Stuffed Onions[109]
Green Salad
Carbonnade[90]
Egg Noodles
Cheesecake

Scotch Ale Vichyssoise[36]
Marinated Paprika Pork Chops[48]
Specialty Potatoes and Cheese[108]
Dilled Carrots[93]
Fresh Fruit Tray

Roasted Garlic Soup[42]
Steamed Green Vegetables
Roast Pork [53]
Mushroom Pilaf[95]
English Trifle

Just Cheese Soup[41]
Apple-Nut Stuffed Pork Chops[63]
Tangy Red Cabbage[100]
Mashed Potatoes
Baked Apples

Ceviche[19]
Coquilles St. Jacques[64]
Steamed Baby Red Potatoes
Buttered Broccoli
Fruit Sherbet

Presentation

The little extras you can add to food upon serving make a big difference in the appeal to your guests. Although they are added at the last minute, they should be an explicit part of your planning, shopping and preparation. Consider some of the following ideas to make your selections more colorful and appetizing.

For soups, you might toss on a few croutons or small crackers just before serving. A sprig of parsley, mint, or watercress can be a colorful addition, as well as slices of green onion tops. Thin slices of carrots or radishes can be floated in the soup. A dollop of yogurt, sour cream, or butter creates a wonderful finishing touch.

Salads become more interesting with a sprinkling of croutons or chopped nuts. A few olives, grapes, or a slice or twist of citrus fruits can also be used. A small quantity of the spicier greens (escarole, watercress, endive, mustard greens, or spinach) lends color and flavor. Also consider a few decoratively cut pieces of almost any vegetable that contrasts with the basic salad. Julienne strips or cubes of cheese or cold meats are a striking complement to a salad.

For main dishes, use fruit cut into wedges or decorative shapes to ring a serving platter. Place a few lemon twists, dill sprigs, or anchovy strips over fish. Place cherry tomatoes, parsley, radishes, watercress, green pepper rings, or mushroom caps around the edge. Meat platters can be adorned with small fresh or cooked fruits such as cherries, kumquats, cranberries, grapes, or pineapple chunks. Sprinkle pimiento pieces, stuffed olives, slivered nuts, or chopped parsley over the main dish. You can also serve the vegetables or side dishes on the main dish platter to provide contrast and color. A separate relish tray of raw vegetables, pickles, and olives is easy to assemble and adds color to the table or buffet area.

The list of potential garnishes is almost endless and doesn't even have to be edible. For example, flower blossoms or ornamental cabbage leaves can create a stunning visual effect. Be creative!

Beer and Food Combinations

When determining which beer to serve with which food, there is only one rule:

There are no rules, only suggestions.

With that in mind, serve the kind of beer you like. If you need some guidelines, you are always safe by offering the type that is contained in the recipe for the course served. Another rule of thumb is that sweeter beers go with sweeter foods. But remember, these are just suggestions—you are the ultimate judge. If it tastes good, do it!

FOOD	BEER SUGGESTION
Fish or white meat	Pilsener
Red meats	Fruity ale or lager
Chicken	Amber or Export lager
Game	Scottish or Belgian ale
Mexican foods and barbecue	Amber lagers
Spicy hot foods	India Pale Ale or Doppelbock[1]
Fried or fatty foods	Well-hopped beers (e.g., alt or IPA)
Sausage and smoked meats	Bock or Dark lager
Shellfish and crustaceans	Porter or Stout
Fruit	Wheat Beer
Nuts or foods with nutty flavor	Brown Ale
Mushrooms	Rauchbier
Raw oysters	Stout (honest! ...try it)
Desserts, cakes, chocolate	Bock, Doppelbock or sweet Stout

You can also serve beers in the same way that certain wines are traditionally used at various points in a meal. For example, a dry, intriguing beer such as a Belgian ale or wheat beer can whet the appetite as an aperitif and a heavy, rich style such as barley-wine or doppelbock makes a wonderful after-dinner drink.

1 Any beer with high alcohol content is suitable. The capsaicin in hot peppers that causes the burning sensation is soluble in alcohol but not water; alcohol will rinse the fiery substance from your tongue more quickly than other beverages.

Party Planning Checklist

These items are a reminder about what to do before you have your one-of-a-kind beer party. They are listed in roughly the order they should be accomplished. There are no set times (e.g., "one day in advance", "one hour before party") because you will have to adapt them to fit your personal schedule. Just make sure you get to all of them before the party.

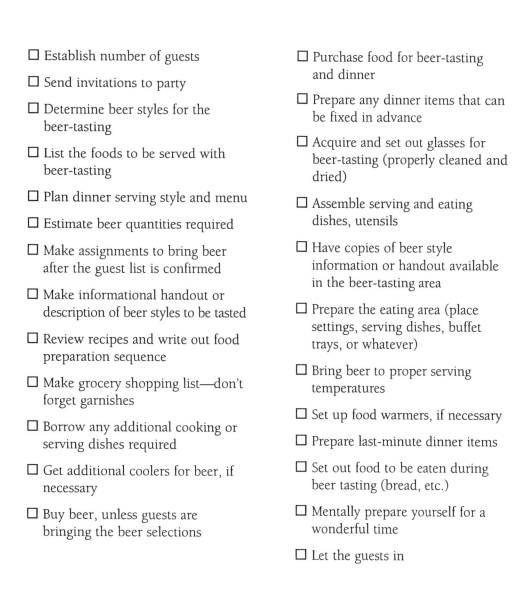

☐ Establish number of guests

☐ Send invitations to party

☐ Determine beer styles for the beer-tasting

☐ List the foods to be served with beer-tasting

☐ Plan dinner serving style and menu

☐ Estimate beer quantities required

☐ Make assignments to bring beer after the guest list is confirmed

☐ Make informational handout or description of beer styles to be tasted

☐ Review recipes and write out food preparation sequence

☐ Make grocery shopping list—don't forget garnishes

☐ Borrow any additional cooking or serving dishes required

☐ Get additional coolers for beer, if necessary

☐ Buy beer, unless guests are bringing the beer selections

☐ Purchase food for beer-tasting and dinner

☐ Prepare any dinner items that can be fixed in advance

☐ Acquire and set out glasses for beer-tasting (properly cleaned and dried)

☐ Assemble serving and eating dishes, utensils

☐ Have copies of beer style information or handout available in the beer-tasting area

☐ Prepare the eating area (place settings, serving dishes, buffet trays, or whatever)

☐ Bring beer to proper serving temperatures

☐ Set up food warmers, if necessary

☐ Prepare last-minute dinner items

☐ Set out food to be eaten during beer tasting (bread, etc.)

☐ Mentally prepare yourself for a wonderful time

☐ Let the guests in

APPENDIX A – BEER JUDGING TERMINOLOGY

When trying to describe the different sensations encountered in the beer-tasting, here are some terms that may be useful. Many of these adjectives are negative, others describe positive characteristics, and some can be either, depending on the beer style being tasted. In any case, beer judges use terms such as these in order to have a common language.

Acidic – a sour taste, like lemon juice

Alcoholic – generally tastes like vodka, with a warming sensation; ethanol-like

Astringent – puckering feel in the mouth (like chewing on a grape skin)

Balance – the term for the flavor resulting from the hops and malt (bitter and sweet) working together; one or the other usually dominates, depending on the particular beer style

Bitter – sensed on the back of the tongue, a taste usually created by hops

Body – the consistency or "thickness" of the beer, ranging from watery to syrupy

Clarity – the transparency of the beer

Clean – lacking any off-flavors

Conditioning – the process of carbonating the beer; "good" conditioning creates a comfortable level of carbonation without generating unintentional flavors

Diacetyl – buttery, butterscotch

DMS (*dimethyl sulfide*) – sweet, corn-like aroma and flavor

Effervescent – having lots of carbonation

Estery – fruit flavors and aromas such as banana, pear, strawberry

Finish – the aftertaste lingering in the mouth after the beer is swallowed

Flat – having little carbonation

Full-bodied – a heavy or thick consistency, sometimes almost syrupy

Hoppy – odor of the hop oil (not bitterness)

Light-struck – having a skunky or catty smell caused by exposure to light

Medicinal – smelling like a band-aid

Metallic – tinny, bloodlike

Nutty – walnut, hazelnut aroma/flavor

Oxidized – smelling of wet cardboard, caused by exposure to oxygen; stale

Phenolic – odors of medicinal, plastic, band-aid, or clove

Salty – sensation on the sides of the tongue towards the front; like table salt

Skunky – the aroma resulting from light affecting the hops elements; light-struck

Sour – sensation on the sides of the tongue towards the back; tart; tasting like vinegar or lemon

Stale – see "Oxidized"

Sweet – sensed on the tip of the tongue; sugary

Sulfur – smell of rotten eggs or burning matches

Thin – watery; having little body

Warming – an alcoholic effect, a mouth sensation similar to drinking vodka

APPENDIX B – SAMPLE JUDGING FORM

BEER JUDGING FORM

Beer Judged _____

CHARACTERISTIC	Maximum Score	Judged Score
APPEARANCE (as appropriate for style)	Color (8) Clarity (6) Head Retention (6)	(20) _____
AROMA/BOUQUET (as appropriate for style)	Malt (10) Hops (10)	(20) _____
FLAVOR (as appropriate for style)	Malt (6) Hops (6) Balance (8) Conditioning (6) Aftertaste (4)	(30) _____
BODY (full or thin as appropriate for style)		(10) _____
OVERALL IMPRESSION		(20) _____
	TOTAL	(100) _____

APPENDIX C – BRAND NAMES AND STYLE REFERENCE

Use this appendix when you want to find beers of a particular style. This listing contains a few of the brands currently representing the styles noted. This is not a complete list; it would take another entire book to list all the beers available, a list which is constantly changing anyway. The exclusion of a particular brand from this appendix represents no judgment about its quality and the listing is in no particular order. In many cases, the beer style represented by a particular brand is subjective; some of the qualities may place it in one category while other characteristics are representative of a different style. There are often shades of grey in categorizing beers and a beer can be legitimately included in several categories—be flexible.

You will quickly notice that the label on the bottle is not always very helpful in identifying the beer style. Porters, stouts, India Pale Ales and wheat beers are usually clearly indicated as such within the name; however, many others are less obvious. When in doubt, find a local liquor store that carries more than the basic American Pilseners and you probably will have found a knowledgeable supplier who can answer questions about beer styles. Add your own notes and brand names to this list as you discover new territories in your great beer adventure. One of the noteworthy stops during your beer exploration should be the Great American Beer Festival®, held annually (usually during October) in Denver, Colorado. Hundreds of brewers exhibit over a thousand different beers in a single tasting event. For more information, contact the Association of Brewers, PO Box 1679, Boulder, CO 80306.

PALE ALE

Samuel Smith's Old Brewery Pale Ale
(The Olde Brewery Tadcaster)

Blue Boar Pale Ale
(Blitz-Weinhard Brewing Co.)

Railyard Ale
(Wynkoop Brewing Co.)

Red Lady Ale
(Crested Butte Brewery and Pub)

90 Shilling
(Odell Brewing Co.)

Bass Pale Ale
(Bass Brewing Ltd.)

Boulder Extra Pale Ale
(Rockies Brewing Co.)

Post Road Pale Ale
(Old Marlborough Brewing Co.)

Pier Pale Ale
(Huntington Beach Beer Co.)

Ranier Ale
(G. Heileman Brewing Co.)

Bridgeport Golden Ale
(Columbia River Brewing Co.)

INDIA PALE ALE

Vail Pale Ale
(Hubcap Brewery and Kitchen)

Blue Heron Pale Ale
(Mendocino Brewing Co.)

Ballantine India Pale Ale
(Falstaff Brewing Co.)

Renegade Red
(Estes Park Brewery)

Oregon I.P.A.
(Oregon Ale and Beer Co.)

McEwan's Export
(Scottish and Newcastle Breweries PLC)

BITTER

Fuller's ESB
(Fuller Smith & Turner PLC)

Young's Special London Ale
(Young and Co. PLC)

Bachelor Bitter
(Deschutes Brewery Inc.)

Belhaven Scottish Ale
(Belhaven Brewery Co. Ltd)

Sawtooth Ale
(Left Hand Brewing Co.)

Four Horsemen Ale
(Mishiwaka Brewing Co.)

Victoria Ave. Amber Ale
(Riverside Brewing Co.)

Whitbread Ale
(Whitbread & Co. PLC)

BROWN ALE

Pyramid Best Brown Ale
(Hart Brewing Co.)

Nut Brown Ale
(Oregon Ale and Beer Co.)

Ball Park Brown Ale
(Breckenridge Brewery)

Tut Brown Ale
(Oasis Brewery)

Ironwood Dark
(Redwood Coast Brewing)

Samuel Smith's Nut Brown Ale
(The Olde Brewery Tadcaster)

Newcastle Brown Ale
(Newcastle Breweries)

BELGIAN ALES

Celis White
(Celis Brewery Inc.)

Belgian Strong Ale
(Pacific Beach Brewhouse)

Lindemans Kriek Lambic
(Brouwerij Lindeman)

Affligem Benedictine Abbey Ale
(Brewery De Smedt)

Trippel Trappist Style Ale
(New Belgium Brewing Co.)

Goudenband
(Liefmans Brewery)

Chimay Ale
(Abbeye de Scourmont)

SCOTCH ALE

MacAndrew's Scotch Ale
(Caledonian Brewery)

Samuel Adams Scotch Ale
(The Boston Beer Co.)

Mogul Madness
(Rogue Ales)

Steelhead Amber
(Steelhead Brewery and Cafe)

McEwan's Scotch Ale
(Scottish and Newcastle Breweries)

Loch Erie Scotch Ale
(Great Lakes Brewing Co.)

PORTER

Anchor Porter
(Anchor Brewing Co.)

Black Jack Porter
(Left Hand Brewing Co.)

Black Butte Porter
(Deschutes Brewery, Inc.)

Cold Cock Winter Porter
(Big Rock Brewery)

Hair of the Dog
(Flying Dog Brewpub)

Moonlight Porter
(Pikes Peak Brewery)

STOUT

Guinness Extra Stout
(Guinness PLC)

Boulder Stout
(Rockies Brewing Co.)

Oatmeal Stout
(Gray Brewing Co.)

Dragon Stout
(Desnoes and Geddes, Ltd)

ABC Extra Stout
(Archipelago Brewing Co.)

Samuel Adams Cream Stout
(The Boston Beer Co.)

IMPERIAL STOUT

Samuel Smith's Imperial Stout
(The Olde Brewery Tadcaster)

Grant's Imperial Stout
(Grant's Ales/Yakima Brewing)

BARLEYWINE

Old Foghorn Barleywine
(Anchor Brewing Co.)

Sierra Nevada Bigfoot Ale
(Sierra Nevada Brewing Co.)

Calistoga "Old Faithful" Barleywine
(Napa Valley Brewing Co.)

Old Nick
(Young and Co's Brewery PLC)

Lagers

PILSENER

Pilsner Urquell
(Pilsner Urquell-Plzen)

Original Coors
(Coors Brewing Co.)

Coors Extra Gold
(Coors Brewing Co.)

Budweiser
(Anheuser-Busch Inc.)

Pabst Genuine Draft
(Pabst Brewing Co.)

Olympia
(Pabst Brewing Co.)

Grain Belt Premium
(Minnesota Brewing Co.)

Lone Star
(Lone Star Brewing Co.)

Lowenbrau
(Miller Brewing Co.)

Signature
(The Stroh Brewery Co.)

Broken Hill Lager
(South Australia Brewing Co. Ltd)

Rolling Rock
(Latrobe Brewing Co.)

Steinlager
(New Zealand Breweries Ltd)

OB
(Oriental Brewing Co. Ltd)

St. Pauli Girl
(St. Pauli Brauerei)

Grolsch
(Grolsch Bierbrouwerijen)

Moretti
(Birra Moretti S.p.A)

Molson
(Molson Breweries of Canada, Ltd.)

33
(Union De Brasseries)

Tuborg
(G. Heileman Brewing Co.)

Kirin
(Kirin Brewery Co., Ltd.)

Kronenbourg
(Kronenbourg Breweries)

Tsingtao
(Tsingtao Brewery Co., Ltd.)

Falstaff
(Falstaff Brewing Co.)

Fosters
(Carlton and United Breweries Ltd.)

Henry Weinhard Private Reserve
(Blitz-Weinhard Brewing Co.)

Miller Lite
(Miller Brewing Co.)

MUNICH HELLES

Dock Street Helles
(Dock Street Brewing Co.)

Hubsch Lager
(Sudwerk Privatbrauerei Hubsch)

Export Gold
(Stoudt Brewing Co.)

Golden Spike Lager
(Tabernash Brewing Co.)

Paulaner Pils
(Paulanerbrau)

BOCK

Pale Bock
(Sierra Nevada Brewing Co.)

Augsburger Bock
(Augsburger Brewing Co.)

Blue River Bock
(Breckenridge Brewery)

Ayinger Maibock
(Privatbrauerei Franz Inskelkammer)

Berghoff Bock
(Berghoff-Huber Brewing Co., Ltd.)

Mai-Bock
(Stoudt Brewing Co.)

DOPPELBOCK

Samuel Adams Double Bock
(The Boston Beer Co.)

DeGroen's Doppelbock
(Baltimore Brewing Co.)

Paulaner Salvator
(Paulanerbrau)

Celebrator
(Privatbrauerei Franz Inskelkammer)

EKU 28 Kulminator
(Actienbrauerei Kulmbach)

Liberator Doppelbock
(Saxer Brewing Co.)

Maximator
(Augustiner Brewery)

AMBER

Saranac Adirondack Amber
(F.X. Matt Brewery)

Oktoberfest
(Coors Brewing Co.)

Ambier Vienna Style
(Ambier Brewing Co.)

Dos Equis
(Cerveceria Moctezuma S.A.)

Rhino Chasers Dark Lager
(Rhino Chasers)

Texfest
(Hubcap Brewery and Kitchen/Dallas)

Market Street Oktoberfest
(Bohannon Brewing Co.)

George Killian's Irish Red
(Coors Brewing Co.)

Seadog Oktoberfest
(Sea Dog Brewing Co.)

DARK LAGER

Michelob Classic Dark
(Anheuser-Busch, Inc.)

Lowenbrau Dark
(Miller Brewing Co.)

Augsburger Dark
(Augsberger Brewing Co.)

Henry Weinhard Special Reserve Dark
(Blitz-Weinhard Brewing Co.)

Berghoff Dark Lager
(Joseph Huber Brewing Co. Inc.)

Black Radish
(Weeping Radish Brewery)

Denargo Lager
(Tabernash Brewing Co.)

Samichlaus[2]
(Brauerei Hurlimann)

EXPORT

Special Export
(G. Heilemann Brewing Co.)

Dortmunder
(Great Lakes Brewing Co.)

Dortmunder Export
(Stoudt Brewing Co.)

Dortmunder Union
(Dortmunder Union-Brauerei)

Kessler Lager
(Montana Beverages Ltd)

Hybrid

ALT

Alaskan Amber
(Alaskan Brewing Co.)

Schmaltz's Alt
(August Schell Brewing Co.)

Ad Astra Ale
(Free State Brewing Co.)

St. Stan's Alt
(St. Stan's Brewing)

Atlantic Amber
(New England Brewing)

2 14% alcohol content makes this unique among all beers and possibly in a class of its own

Samuel Adams Boston Stock Ale
(The Boston Beer Co.)

Wild Horse Ale
(Great Basin Brewing Co.)

CREAM ALE

Genesee Cream Ale
(Genesee Brewing Co. Inc.)

Canyon Cream Ale
(Eddie McStiff's)

Holy Cow! Cream Ale
(Holy Cow! Casino, Cafe and Brewery)

Little Kings Cream Ale
(Hudepohl-Schoenling)

WHEAT BEERS

Tabernash Weiss
(Tabernash Brewing Co.)

Samuel Adams Dark Wheat
(The Boston Beer Co.)

Buck Wheat
(Champion Brewing Co.)

Whitewater Wheat Ale
(Great Divide Brewing Co.)

Wit
(Spring Street Brewing Co.)

STEAM BEER

Anchor Steam Beer
(Anchor Brewing Co.)

SPECIALTY

Horizon Honey Ale
(High Point Brewing Corp.)

Katcher's Rye
(H.C. Berger Brewing Co.)

Rauchenfels Steinbier
(Rauchenfels Steinbierbrauerei)

Oregon Honey Beer
(Portland Brewing Co.)

McMahon's Potato Ale
(Minnesota Brewing Co.)

River City Rye Ale
(River City Brewing Co.)

Honey Basil Ale
(Bison Brewing Co.)

RAUCHBIER

Alaskan Smoked Porter
(Alaskan Brewing Co.)

Dixie Holy Smoke
(Dixie Brewing Co.)

Smoked Bawdy
(Pike Place Brewery)

Holy Smoke
(Marin Brewing Co.)

HERB BEER

Juju Ginger Ale
(Left Hand Brewing Co.)

Oldenberg Holy Ginger Red Ale
(Oldenberg Brewing Co.)

Oldenberg Special Spice Ale
(Oldenberg Brewing Co.)

FRUIT BEER

Pyramid Apricot Ale
(Hart Brewing Inc.)

Blueberry Ale
(Oasis Brewery)

Passion Pale
(Alameda Tied House)

Georgia Peach Wheat
(Helenboch Brewery/Friends Brewing)

Brewberry Pale
(Pacific Tap and Grill)

Raspberry Wheat
(Rubicon Brewing Co.)

Black Dog Honey Raspberry Ale
(Black dog)

Raspberry Wheat
(Heavenly Daze Brewery)

Bluebeery Ale
(Marin Brewing Co.)

Beartooth Cranberry Lager
(Beartooth Brewing Co.)

CHRISTMAS BEER

Our Special Ale
(Anchor Brewing Co.)

Sierra Nevada Celebration Ale
(Sierra Nevada Brewing Co.)

Winterfest
(Coors Brewing Co.)

Yule-Tied
(Redwood Coast Brewery)

Hoppy Holidaze
(Marin Brewing Co.)

Winterhook
(Redhook Ale Brewery, Inc.)

CHILI BEER

Sigda's Green Chili Beer
(Coopersmith's Pub and Brewing)

Cave Creek Chili Beer
(Black Mountain Brewery)

Taos Green Chili Beer
(Eske's Brewpub)

Cerveza Chilibeso
(Great Basin Brewing Co.)

ALPHABETICAL INDEX

BEER INGREDIENT INDEX

Each recipe is grouped in this index based on the beer style recommended as an ingredient. If several beer options are referenced in the recipe, it will be listed in this index under all applicable styles. But remember, these are only suggestions—experiment with what you think will taste good!

Ales

Lagers

MAIN INGREDIENT INDEX

This index provides a listing of the recipes based on the main ingredient(s). If there are two or more predominant ingredients, the recipe will be found more than once in the listing. You can look in your refrigerator or pantry shelves, see what's there, then consult this index to find a suitable answer to your question, "What can I make with this stuff?" Or use this index take advantage of sales in your local grocery stores.

PREPARATION TIME INDEX

The recipes are grouped in this index based on the time it would take to prepare that dish. The time used for comparison is the actual time spent preparing the food, but does not include any time which doesn't require your attention to the food (i.e., marinating, baking, thawing, chilling). For example, a recipe for a marinated meat which takes a few minutes to prepare the marinade and then eight hours for the meat to sit in the marinade will be listed under "Quick." A meal that takes less than 20 minutes of the cook's attention is considered "Quick," a "Lengthy" preparation time is more than 40 minutes and an "Average" recipe is in-between. When planning a menu for your dinner party, make sure you read the recipe and estimate the total elapsed time from start to finish.

QUICK

AVERAGE